REALIZATION OF ONENESS

REALIZATION OF ONENESS

The Practice of Spiritual Healing by Joel S. Goldsmith

Edited by Lorraine Sinkler

THE CITADEL PRESS
SECAUCUS, N.J.

Third paperbound printing
Copyright © 1967 by Emma Goldsmith
All rights reserved
Published by Citadel Press
A division of Lyle Stuart, Inc.
120 Enterprise Ave., Secaucus, N. J. 07094
In Canada: George J. McLeod Limited
73 Bathurst St., Toronto, Ont.
Manufactured in the United States of America
ISBN 0-8065-0453-6

Except the Lord build the house,
they labour in vain that build it.

—Psalm 127

Illumination dissolves all material ties and binds men together with the golden chains of spiritual understanding; it acknowledges only the leadership of the Christ; it has no ritual or rule but the divine, impersonal universal Love, no other worship than the inner Flame that is ever lit at the shrine of Spirit. This union is the free state of spiritual brotherhood. The only restraint is the discipline of Soul; therefore, we know liberty without license; we are a united universe without physical limits, a divine service to God without ceremony or creed. The illumined walk without fear—by Grace.

—The Infinite Way

Contents

REALIZATION OF ONENESS

1) Pure Being

For thousands of years, man has held God responsible for the evils of this world, believing that He rewards and punishes, that He is responsible for the accidents, diseases, and disasters of this earth, that tornadoes, cyclones, hurricanes, and tidal waves are acts of God. For thousands of years, too, man has been commanded: "And thou shalt love the Lord thy God with all thine heart, and with all thy soul, and with all thy might."[1] But is it possible for a person to love a God who at one moment may reward and bless and who at the next moment, for no reason whatsoever, may visit horrible diseases, accidents, and death upon him?

EDITOR'S NOTE: The material in *Realization of Oneness* first appeared in the form of letters sent to students of The Infinite Way throughout the world as an aid to the revelation and unfoldment of the transcendental Consciousness through a deeper understanding of Scripture and the principles of The Infinite Way.
[1] Deuteronomy 6:5.

There is no way to "love the Lord thy God" except by understanding and becoming convinced that evil does not have its rise in God, and that neither sin, disease, accident, death, famine, storm, nor drought—none of these—comes forth from God. Only in the degree that we can disassociate God from being the cause of evil can we become free of it, because the evil in our experience stems from the belief that God, in some way, is responsible for it.

This misconception as to the nature of God was evident in the earliest days of the Hebrew people when they turned hopefully to God for their blessings, but at the same time feared His cursing. This is well illustrated in the story of Noah and the Ark. Because Noah was a good and upright man, God was going to save him, and He, therefore, instructed him to build an ark and fill it with all manner of beasts, with cattle, creeping things, and fowl with which to provide for him and his family. But the same God who was going to do that for Noah was going "to destroy all flesh, wherein is the breath of life." [2]

Is it possible that Noah was the only holy or righteous man on earth? Even were that true and all other men wicked, from whence would come their capacity to be evil? Where but from God, and if from God, why, then, would God punish them? And if God did not give man the capacity to sin, where would he receive this capacity, since God is his Father, his creative Principle, and the Source of all there is?

Perhaps in those days the people did not have the wisdom to raise such questions. They had only the darkness of superstition and ignorance and, therefore, they blessed God when He blessed them and cursed Him when disaster overtook them, believing that good and evil came forth from God.

With the advent of that spiritual light which was embodied in the consciousness of Jesus Christ in its fullness, we are presented with a different God, a God in whom there is no dark-

2 Genesis 6:17.

ness, a God too pure to behold iniquity, a God who demands of us that we be so pure that we even forgive our enemies and pray for those who despitefully use us. The God Jesus gave to the world is a God that demands of us that we hold no one in condemnation, that we visit no punishment on the sinner.

IS MAN MORE LOVING AND JUST THAN GOD?

Is not God greater than we are? Is not the love of God greater than any love that we can express? Are not the wisdom and the justice of God greater than the wisdom and justice of man? To ascribe evil in any form to God is to make God lower than man, for of man it is demanded, "Be ye therefore perfect, even as your Father which is in heaven is perfect." [3] No one would ever consider any man perfect who visited sin, disease, or death on another—not for any reason! Even in this modern day when civilization is still in its infancy, man is developing enough love and understanding so that capital punishment is gradually being eliminated. If man can be that just and considerate, how much more compassionate and understanding must God be!

In some instances, this same consideration is now being extended to international relationships, so that today instead of wreaking vengeance on a country which has waged war against us we help bolster its tottering economy and strengthen its financial structure. If nations can do that, how much more can and does God do? How much more of love, intelligence, life, and purity is there in God! To ascribe less than perfection to God is sinful. It is blasphemy.

Many of the discords from which we suffer have their roots in the universal belief that God visits these evils upon us, either to punish us, to teach us a lesson, or for some other reason. There are those who even believe what is often preached at

[3] Matthew 5:48.

some funeral services, "God has called this dear one home."
The "calling home" has often come about by way of cancer,
consumption, or an automobile accident. It is blasphemous to
believe that God operates in such a fashion. Nevertheless, the
universal belief is that God is responsible for our troubles, and
you and I are suffering from our ignorant and unconscious
acceptance of that belief. We may not be aware of this, but it is
so ingrained in consciousness that we suffer from it.

To begin to set ourselves free from the penalties of universal
beliefs, we must release God from all responsibility for the sins,
diseases, deaths, droughts, lacks, and limitations of this world.
We must honor our Father which is in heaven. We must love
the Lord our God with all our heart and with all our soul in
the realization that He is too pure to behold iniquity or to
cause it. He is the very light of the world, and in Him is no
darkness at all.

ONENESS OF GOD AND MAN

When that conviction becomes bone of our bone and flesh of
our flesh and when we have a God wholly good, we ourselves
then are wholly good, for "I and my Father are one.[4] . . . Son,
thou art ever with me, and all that I have is thine."[5] All the
qualities we now attribute to God—all the purity, goodness,
justice, love, and forgiveness—are in reality qualities of man,
for God and man are one, just as the glass and the tumbler are
one. What is the nature of the tumbler? Is there a tumbler or is
there just glass? Is the tumbler merely a name for the form as
which the glass is appearing? Glass is the essence of the tumbler; glass is its quality. How strong is the tumbler? As strong
as the glass of which it is made. How beautiful is the tumbler?
As beautiful as the glass of which it is made.

[4] John 10:30.
[5] Luke 15:31.

And what of man and his relationship to God? Is not man but the form or the temple, and God the essence of his being? Is it any more possible to separate God from man than glass from the tumbler? Is not God the substance of man's life, of his mind, of his Soul, and of his Spirit? Is not even his body the temple of God?

Once we perceive that oneness is the true relationship of God and man and, at the same time, perceive the pure nature of God in whom there is no propensity for evil, man is also recognized as pure and upright in whom there likewise is no propensity or capacity for evil. Before we can wipe sin, disease, death, accident, poverty, or injustice off this earth, we must first remove it from God. Then we shall have a universe showing forth God's glory, and God's glory can be only perfection itself.

"He that hath seen me hath seen the Father[6] . . . [for] I and my Father are one."[7] The Father is greater than we are because the Father is the substance and essence of being, and we are but the form which appears in infinite variety. Just as the glass is greater than the form it takes and can be molded into a tumbler, a sauce-dish, or a pepper shaker, with the glass always retaining the quality, essence, character, and nature of whatever form it takes, so is God the nature, essence, activity, and the law unto every form, including man' animal, plant, and mineral.

The nature of man, then, is the nature of God expressed individually, and this man, therefore, must be the image and likeness of God, the showing forth of God. For man to be holy, God must be holy; for man to love his enemies, God must have no other feeling than love; for man to be forgiving, God must express no condemnation, no judgment, no punishment.

Is it not clear, then, that the beginning of freedom for you

6 John 14:9.
7 John 10:30.

and for me is to have God wholly good, God from whom can come forth nothing but Spirit, eternality, and justice? God looked on what He had made, and behold, He found it very good. The goodness that is in God is innate in the goodness of His creation.

But if we claim that God is wholly good, that still has no effect on our life as long as we are separate and apart from God. God may be wholly good, but we do not share in that goodness until we can perceive our oneness with God as heir of God and joint-heir to all the heavenly riches, and accept the promise, "Son . . . all that I have is thine." Unless we can see that oneness, it will be like believing that Jesus was wholly good, that he was the son of God, but that we are not. What good is Jesus' perfection if it is not also our perfection? What good would come from God's being perfect, if you and I were something separate and apart from God, subject to other influences?

But we are not something separate and apart from God. "I and my Father are one," and in that relationship of oneness the perfection of God is our perfection, and God's freedom from the capacity to sin or to suffer disease, lack, or limitation is also our freedom. Whatever goodness is being made manifest through us is God's goodness; whatever immortality is the immortality of God; whatever of love or of justice is the love or the justice of God; whatever of intelligence is God's.

"His understanding is infinite." [8] But what good is that to you or to me unless we are one with Him? In that relationship of oneness, His infinite understanding becomes the measure and the capacity of our understanding. Only in oneness can that happen, and so the moment we declare the infinite, perfect, spiritual nature of God, we are also declaring the perfection of our own being.

8 Psalm 147:5.

GOD IS FOREVER POURING ITSELF FORTH

In order to free ourselves from the limitations of human sense, we must understand the nature of God. God is not a power over evil, and we have no power over evil. To believe that God is a power over evil is to believe that evil has an existence, and then we either must believe God to be the cause and creator of it or we must accept another cause and creator, and the acceptance of any other cause or creator does away with Omnipotence, Omniscience, and Omnipresence.

We must have only one Creator, and that One without capacity for sin or any evil. Then we do not need a power over sin, disease, or death because these have no existence in God, and if they do not exist in God, they do not exist. They can exist only as beliefs in the human consciousness that believes in two powers, even believes that God has within Itself [9] two powers: the power to reward and the power to punish, the power to give and the power to withhold.

How we "finitize" God! How we limit God! How we make God just a bigger edition of mortals when we make Him something that has the power to give or withhold sunshine, something that has the power to give or withhold crops! Such a belief places God in the same category as mortals. God is not like that at all. God cannot give sunshine, and God cannot withhold sunshine. God cannot give us life, and God cannot give us death. God *is* eternal life, and His life is the life of our being. He does not give it: *He is it.*

God does not give us purity. God is our Soul, and the Soul of God being pure, our Soul is pure. God does not give us wis-

[9] In the spiritual literature of the world, the varying concepts of God are indicated by the use of such words as "Father," "Mother," "Soul," "Spirit," "Principle," "Love," or "Life." Therefore, in this book, the author has used the pronouns "He" and "It," or "Himself" and "Itself," interchangeably in referring to God.

dom. God is wisdom, but being infinite, God is our wisdom. There is no giving, and there is no withholding. There is only *"Is-ing."* If there were a God-life and our life, God-life might be immortal and ours mortal; but if God is infinite, God is infinite life, and that means your life and my life.

THERE IS NO GOD IN EVIL

To know Him aright is life eternal, and as we begin to know God as complete, pure Being, without any capacity to wipe out a nation or punish sinners, God that cannot visit disease on innocent persons or even on guilty persons, God that does not permit conditions of war or poverty, we have freed ourselves, because much of the cause of evil in our lives is the belief that in some way God is the cause of it, the author, the creator, and the maintainer of it.

When we come to know God aright, we have a God that we can love with all our heart and with all our soul, because we can look upon this world with its injustices, sins, and disasters and be thankful that there is no God in any of the evils besetting mankind. When we have removed God from them, we have removed the substance from them, and they begin to destroy themselves. They begin to dissolve.

God is never in any form of force—"not by might, nor by power, but by my spirit." [10] There is no evil where My[11] Spirit is, for where My Spirit is, there is liberty.

The world must awaken. It must awaken to the realization of the true nature of God in order to remove the cause of evil. Some persons believe that wars are righteous, and that God is on one side or another. God on the side of people out killing! God on the side of people murdering innocent men and women and children! God could not be in a war. God is not in

10 Zechariah 4:6.
11 The word "My," capitalized, refers to God.

the whirlwind; God is not in the storm: God is in the still small voice.

OVERCOMING IDOLATRY

When we come face to face with our fears, what do we find? We are usually fearing some person, thing, or condition, or, on the other hand, very often we may be worshiping some person, thing, or condition. Habbakuk had a word for it:

> What profiteth the graven image that the maker thereof hath graven it; the molten image, and a teacher of lies, that the maker of his work trusteth therein, to make dumb idols?
>
> Woe unto him that saith to the wood, Awake; to the dumb stone, Arise, it shall teach! Behold, it is laid over with gold and silver, and there is no breath at all in the midst of it.
>
> But the Lord is in his holy temple: let all the earth keep silence before him.
>
> Habbakuk 2:18-20

Many persons place their hopes and fears in persons or things. It may be in gold or silver; it may be in land or in securities, or even in social security; but when hope, ambition, and confidence are in something external, that is nothing more nor less than idolatry. All this disappears when we understand that the nature of God is the nature of individual being; and, therefore, there is no need to want some particular person, thing, or circumstance, for we embody our good. "Son, thou art ever with me, and all that I have is thine." All that *I* [12] have! Let us not worry about what somebody else has! "All that *I* have is thine."

In the realization that God is our very own being, how can we fear, love, or hate gold or silver, germs or poisons, bullets or

[12] The word *"I,"* italicized, refers to God.

bombs? How can we fear that God or God's being can be destroyed? And is not God's being the essence and substance of our being? We are the tumbler, the form, but God is the essence and substance even of our bodies. We need not fear what mortals can do to us. We need not fear what mortal circumstances or conditions can do to us. God is the essence of our being, and in Him there is no darkness. Therefore, in that of which we are formed, there is no capacity for negative activity of any form or nature. But, if we do not know the nature of God, how can we know the nature of our perfect Self? If we do not credit God with being pure, how then can we be pure? We can be no more pure than our Source, our Essence, our Substance.

When we see evil in any form—in our own experience, in the experience of the world or of our neighbor—we can smile within ourselves as we realize:

> *There is no God in this. This never had its rise in God: it has no God-substance, no God-law, no God-life, no God-being. It is the "arm of flesh,"* [13] *nothingness.*[14]

This immediately takes from evil its sting. We let it dissolve of itself and disappear from sight by removing from it that which gives it life, that is, the belief that it is of God, that it emanates from God, and that God is responsible for it. But if there is no evil in God, there is no evil at all for God is the source of all creation. We need only to look at any situation and realize: "There is no God in this, no power to sustain it,

---

[13] II Chronicles 32:8.
[14] The italicized portions of this book are spontaneous meditations that have come to the author during periods of uplifted consciousness and are not in any sense intended to be used as affirmations, denials, or formulas. They have been inserted in this book from time to time to serve as examples of the free flowing of the Spirit. As the reader practices the Presence, he, too, in his exalted moments, will receive ever new and fresh inspirations as the outpouring of the Spirit.

and no law of God to maintain it. There is no power but God."
Then it must dissolve and disappear.

This removes idolatry. It prevents us from loving, fearing, or
hating that which has form, because we know that the real
essence of all form is God. Any erroneous form that may appear has no existence except in the belief in two powers, or
except in the belief that God caused it. Once we remove God as
the cause, foundation, and source of evil, we have begun its
dissolution.

As human beings, we are living a life separate and apart
from God, and as long as we do that, there is certain to be
some good and some evil. This is because we have no clear-cut
principle by which to live. We have not grasped the meaning
of the omnipresence of God. We do not understand that where
God is, *I* am, that the place whereon we stand is holy ground,
that the presence of God is within us, that there is a God
"closer . . . than breathing, and nearer than hands and feet," [15]
and that wherever we go God goes with us. If we mount up to
heaven, we find God there; if we make our bed in hell, there,
too, we find God; if we "walk through the valley of the
shadow of death," [16] God is there

But what is the nature of this Presence that is with us? Is the
presence of God going to reward us? Is It going to punish us?
Is It going to heal us? Is It going to visit iniquity upon us
"unto the third and fourth generation," [17] or is this God that is
with us a wholly good influence, a perfect influence, an influence for freedom, joy, and for infinite good in our life?

The first step on the spiritual path is to become aware of
God's presence, to live always as if God were bearing witness
with us, as if God were going before us. Once that is attained,
our next great unfoldment must be the nature of God because

[15] Alfred, Lord Tennyson. *The Higher Pantheism,* Stanza 6.
[16] Psalm 23:4.
[17] Exodus 20:5.

this is the step that brings freedom and release from what the Master called "this world." [18] To know God as that pure Being in whom evil has no rise, no source, no foundation, no cause, and no power is to live in freedom because if He is not the cause of evil, it has no cause, for God alone is law, life, substance, activity, and being.

This makes it possible to overcome idolatry, because when we have a God of purity, there is nothing to fear, there is no person or thing which can have any qualities of evil derived from God. Anything derived from mortal consciousness is not of God, and therefore not power. So when we behold injustices, inequalities, sins, persecutions, and revilings, our answer should be, "So what! Be not afraid! None of this emanates from God, and therefore, you, Pilate, 'couldest have no power at all against me.' [19] The only power that you have is that which is derived from God. What is not derived from God is not power."

CHRISTHOOD AROUND THE GLOBE

Every kind of evil in international affairs will be dissolved, but it will be dissolved because there are now persons on earth knowing that these evils have no existence in God; and therefore, they have no existence. They do not have their rise in God; therefore, they have no power. Just ten righteous men in a city can save it—a few hundred or a few thousand who can face every situation of human experience in the realization, "You do not have your rise in God, so you are not power. You have no foundation in God; you have no power. You have no law of God to maintain or sustain you; you have no power."

Then rest! Rest in His word. Rest in this Word; abide in this

18 John 18:36.
19 John 19:11.

Word; dwell "in the secret place of the most High," [20] always looking out at these forms or formations without hate, love, or fear, knowing that if they do not have their rise in God, they have no substance, no law, no cause, no effect.

As we are able to prove a degree of freedom from these universal beliefs in our individual experience, we begin to free our neighbor—not because he asks us to pray for him, but because when we see his sins or his diseases, we know within ourselves: "This has no rise in God, no foundation in God; it has no law of God. Be not afraid."

Such a response to evil makes of every person an influence in the world because, even though he cannot physically be present all over the world, by his influence he will be imparting the truth of the all-power of God and the nonpower of evil, so that he will be a part of a circle of Christhood around the globe. What is a circle of Christhood except a circle of those who realize that evil does not have its rise in God and, therefore, it has no law and no substance to sustain it? By abiding in that truth, they watch it as it dissolves and disappears.

That is the circle of Christhood: those who do not accept evil as real, because they do not accept evil as having a foundation in God.

The Secret of The Infinite Way

The secret of The Infinite Way is revealed in the truth that the only God there is, is Consciousness, and since God is the one Consciousness, this is the Consciousness of individual man and, therefore, the Consciousness of individual man is his creator, maintainer, and sustainer. Out of the Consciousness of

[20] Psalm 91:1.

individual man must come all that is necessary for his fulfillment.

The Master, repeating the revelation of Moses, "*I AM THAT I AM,*" [21] gave *I* as the secret name of God: *I* am the bread, the meat, the wine, and the water; "I am the resurrection.[22] . . . I am the way, the truth, and the life." [23] So you must see that even if you destroy this temple, whether it is the temple of your body, of your home, of your family, of your fortune, or of your business—whatever temple you may destroy —*I* will raise it up again because *I* is Consciousness, or God.

When man turns anywhere other than to the Withinness of his own being for life, supply, harmony, health, wholeness, completeness, success, wisdom, purity, or any other imaginable thing or thought, he is turning to where it is not, and the result is that there are persons of every religion and denomination praying in churches throughout the world. How many of such prayers are answered? And why is this? Because the prayers are addressed to a Presence and Power separate and apart from the one praying; whereas if the prayer were addressed to God in the inner sanctuary of his own being, in secrecy, where the Master told us to address it; and then, were the person to pray not for *things*—not for his life, or what he should eat or drink, but pray for a realization of the nature of the kingdom of God —then all these *things* would be added unto him from within the divine Consciousness which is his own being.

Why does Isaiah say, "Is there a God beside me? yea, there is no God; I know not any"? [24] This "Me" [25] is *I,* and this *I* is the infinite, divine Consciousness of my individual being. Therefore, I am not Its master, nor do I have the wisdom to tell It what I want, or when, how much, or how little; nor do I have

21 Exodus 3:14.
22 John 11:25.
23 John 14:6.
24 Isaiah 44:8.
25 The word "Me," capitalized, refers to God.

the wisdom to direct It to anyone else, because the *I* of me is infinite, divine Consciousness, the All-knowing.

As revealed in Scripture, God is in the "still small voice," [26] and so the only form of true prayer is the inner listening ear. It is for this reason that the most important part of our work in The Infinite Way is meditation, because no one has access to the inner sanctuary of his being, his inner consciousness, except through the listening ear. Meditation is the practice of listening for this still small voice, creating within one's self practically a vacuum in which the presence of God can announce Itself.

Students complain that this is difficult. It is difficult largely because it has not been practiced for hundreds of years, and they must now learn something that has been out of consciousness for generations. That is not easy. If students are seeking an easy path, they are not going to find it in The Infinite Way because The Infinite Way has no other access to the kingdom of God than through meditation.

Any degree of good that a student may receive from a practitioner or a teacher is only of temporary help because it is still true that while a Moses can lead his flock *to* the Promised Land, he cannot take them *into* it. That, they must do for themselves. The Master later confirmed this in his statement, "If I go not away, the Comforter will not come unto you." [27] By "Comforter," he meant that which completes your demonstration, that which provides you with the ultimate comfort, the full peace, and the fulfillment of your destiny. And even as it came to the Master, as it came to Moses, Elijah, and Isaiah, so must it come to you.

Remember that not even Jesus took his disciples into the kingdom of heaven. He left them on earth and told them to remain in that consciousness until they were imbued from on High with spiritual power, a clear indication that the Master

[26] I Kings 19:12.
[27] John 16:7.

felt that his disciples had not yet attained the necessary vision to know how to meditate properly and draw forth from the Father within all that He had been teaching them, which, in the last analysis, must come from the Father within, and not from any external source.

Why do you think the Master made it so clear that the kingdom of God is neither "Lo here! or, lo there!" [28] and that it is not to be found in holy mountains or in holy temples, but rather it is within you? And why do you think that the mystical poet, Robert Browning, had the vision that Truth is within you and that you must open out a way for the imprisoned splendor to escape? How are you going to do this without meditation, without creating within yourself a vacuum through the listening ear, so that from this divine Consciousness can come forth your meat, wine, bread, water, resurrection, and even "restore to you the years that the locust hath eaten." [29]

If you have not learned from the message of The Infinite Way that the only good you are ever going to receive is from within your own consciousness, then you have failed to perceive the nature of its message and mission, which is that God constitutes your consciousness and that through meditation you must draw forth from within your own consciousness the allness and the fulfillment of life.

Infinity and immortality are made manifest as the consciousness of the individual, and the name of this divine Consciousness, which is our individual consciousness, is *I*. You must understand that you are not to direct this *I*, enlighten It, plead with It, or try to be a master of It, but that you are to submit and yield yourself servant to the *I* of your own being, so that your prayer is that *I* fulfill Itself as your individual experience, that *I* be the Grace which is your sufficiency, and then *let* this *I*

28 Luke 17:21.
29 Joel 2:25.

which is your true Selfhood govern your life in Its own way.

When you then go into prayer and meditation, there must be no preconceived idea as to what you want or how you wish your prayer to be answered. There must be a complete yielding as you daily realize, "Not my will, but thine, be done." [30] Do not go to God with your thoughts and do not try to have God fulfill your way, because you will fail. You must go to God, the divine Consciousness of your own being, the very *I* which you are, with this prayer: "Reveal to me Thy way, Thy will, Thy thought, and this, then, will be my way, my will, and my thought."

Now we come to the revelation of The Infinite Way that must startle those who are not prepared for it. Nevertheless, until this revelation has been discerned, the fruitage of the Message cannot fully come into the experience of an individual. I ask you to look at a tree. It does not make any difference what tree you look at, but look at some tree. You know that from this tree seeds develop and that these seeds drop into the ground at the foot of the tree, or are carried away by birds and dropped into the ground somewhere else, and that, in time, these seeds become new trees.

As you look at the tree, if possible, visualize a seed still on the tree, and then watch the seed drop into the ground. While you are doing this, remember that the life of the tree is the life of the seed. When the seed drops into the ground, the life of the tree is still the life of the seed, and when the seed gets into the earth and breaks open and becomes a root, the life of the tree, which was the life of the seed, is now the life of the root. The root now grows up into a tree, and it is still the life of the tree, which was the life of the seed, which is now the life of the tree. While, to sight, you have tree, seed, and tree, actually you have only one life manifesting itself as a tree, a seed, and the new tree—always the same life.

[30] Luke 22:42.

In using the tree as an example of Life expressing Itself, what I want you to see is that you are not the tree, that you never were the seed, and that you are not the new tree: you are the life of that first tree, of the seed, and of the next tree. Therefore, your life has been, and is, continuous since "before Abraham was." [31] As a matter of fact, the life of God is your life; therefore, your life coexisted with God in the beginning, and down through all the ages of fathers, mothers, grandfathers, grandmothers, great-grandparents, and on into infinity, but always it is the one Life which *I AM*.

Actually, therefore, *I* am the life of all my ancestors, and *I* will be the life of all my children, grandchildren, great-grandchildren, and great-great-grandchildren, because it will be the same life appearing as me, as the seed, as my child, as his seed, and as his child. Always it will be *I* appearing *as*. This is my immortality, the immortality of my life manifested as many forms in many generations.

When you look in the mirror, please remember that you are not seeing "you": you are seeing your body, just as, when you look at the tree, you are not seeing a tree at all: you are seeing the body of a tree, for the tree itself is life. So the Self of you, which is *I AM,* is the real you, and the body is only the form, and as you drop a seed, it will still be your life. Then, as your child appears, it will be the life which *you* are, appearing as another form, and therefore, you are immortalized in your children, and as your children, all the way down to the end of time. The secret is, " 'I will never leave thee, nor forsake thee.' [32] *I* will be with thee unto the end of time, for *I* am thee."

Since there is but one Consciousness, and therefore, there can be but one *I*, remember that *I* am not only the life of my children and the life of my parents, *I* am the life of my neighbors, of their cats, their dogs, and their crops, and *I* am the life of my

31 John 8:58.
32 Hebrews 13:5.

enemies. It is for this reason that the Master taught us to forgive seventy times seven, to pray for our enemies, and to do
unto others as we would have others do unto us. The reason i
that anything you do to another you are doing unto yourself
because there is but one Self, and *I* am that Self.

Be assured that even the money that you give to benevo-
lences is only being transferred from your right-hand pocket to
your left-hand pocket, because *I* is the only Selfhood, and
therefore, what you give never leaves you. This is the bread
that you cast on the water of life which comes back to you.
The forgiveness that you give to those who have offended you
is the forgiving of yourself because there is no other Self than *I*
AM, and without the forgiving of others, there can be no forgiving of yourself, for *I* am the only other.

When you pray for your enemies, you are praying for yourself. You are doing unto others as you would have others do
unto you, and the reason is that the enemy is yourself. Therein
is one of the great secrets of mysticism. The twelve disciples of
Jesus were not men: they were facets of his own consciousness.
The Master embodied within himself the qualities of Peter,
John, and Judas. Like it or not, this is the mystical truth.

You may think that you have loving friends and unloving
ones, but you have neither. These loving friends and unloving
friends are qualities of your own consciousness, which are you
being externalized. It is as if you were to draw pictures of
twelve men and women, any twelve you like, and when you
had drawn them, you may be assured that you would have
drawn your own concepts of manhood and womanhood, and
nothing else, and there would be no use in blaming anybody
for how your men and women looked.

So you have drawn the pictures of your loving and of your
unloving friends, and they are ideas in your mind. You have
projected them, and they are your images in thought. The only
way they will ever be changed is by changing your concepts of

manhood and womanhood, and the higher the ideal of manhood and womanhood you attain, the higher manifestation of men and women will be drawn into your experience.

Across the Desk

This comes to you from London as the year 1963 draws to a close—the most momentous year of my work since receiving my initiation and instructions in The Infinite Way in 1946. This year, 1963, the word came to me to take our students from metaphysics to mysticism.

My personal life has had many difficult periods since my first spiritual experience in 1929 because that experience lifted me into the fourth-dimensional consciousness, and yet I had to live in two worlds in order to carry on first a healing ministry and then both healing and teaching. Except when done in absolute silence, spiritual healing and teaching are conducted out from the ordinary consciousness, and yet the inspiration is always from above. To live in two worlds has always been difficult for me, but it has been necessary as there must be the metaphysical consciousness on earth before the mystical can be attained.

In 1959, I was instructed to give a full year of classes on the basic principles of The Infinite Way and then begin raising up the son of God in man. Finally, this year the word came to lift our students out of the metaphysical into the mystical, and this mission was immediately undertaken.

First, I gave instructions to ministers and Infinite Way teachers, instructions which are contained in five teaching tapes which have now become available to all students. These give the principles which for all time will establish students on a firm foundation for healing and teaching The Infinite Way.

Regardless of whether anyone ever heals or teaches others, this is his foundation for spiritual unfoldment.

Then, with students coming to Hawaii from near and far, I began the transition in consciousness for our students from the metaphysical to the mystical. This work is embodied in the three *1963 Princess Kaiulani Sunday Series* tape recordings and the nine *1963 Kailua Private Class* tapes.

What measure of Grace these bring to anyone is wholly dependent on the measure of dedication he brings to the study, and especially to the meditation and practice. You may accept this as a major spiritual principle: you receive only in proportion to what you bring or give. There is no such thing as *getting* spiritually. What you bring or give to any spiritual life is reflected back to you.

A Parenthesis in Eternity[33] is given us at this particular time to make it clear to you and to the world that the day of spiritual grace has come upon the world. Furthermore, ever since its publication, *The Contemplative Life*[34] has been my Infinite Way bible. I know that as you come to understand this book, it will be your bible, too.

Regardless of the progress, or lack of it, in our students, the Message is now in consciousness, and its purpose is being served. The unfoldment of truth in consciousness is not dependent on man, but when truth is released, it serves the purpose whereunto it is sent. God's will is being done on earth.

If they wish, our students can be instruments of God's grace, but whether they are or not, be assured that God has sent His word into consciousness, and it is now being established and will bear fruit, rich and ripe and abundant.

[33] By the author (New York: Harper and Row, 1963; London: George Allen and Unwin, 1964).
[34] By the author (New York: The Julian Press, 1963; London: L. N. Fowler and Co. Ltd., 1963).

2) *Release Man*

Freedom is the normal and natural state of the son of God. The person who has realized his spiritual nature and identity and who lives by the Spirit cannot be limited in any way. There is no way to confine spiritual being. On the other hand, a human being can never escape slavery because slavery is the natural state of the human being. A human being is destined to be in slavery throughout all his days; he can never know freedom. Therefore, the only hope a human being has is to rise out of his humanhood.

The dignity of the individual demands freedom—freedom from political and religious domination, wage domination, from every form of domination, including the most enslaving of all, the domination of the body. Even those who have achieved a measure of freedom from all other forms of slavery finally must acknowledge that they are slaves of the body.

They live within its confines, and the body is a hard taskmaster. The body tells us when it is healthy and when it is sick. It tells us how much walking we can do and how much running. It tells us how many hours a day we can work.

We seem to have no control over the body. It has control over us: we obey its mandates and are limited by its demands. This is not natural; this is not normal; and this is not the birthright of man. This condition has been imposed upon the human race that lives in ignorance of the principles that will make it free.

Freedom, however, does not come by fighting evil. It does not come by overpowering error, nor does it come by appealing to some unknown God to come down out of the sky to rescue us from our vile prisons. It does not come through warfare of any name or nature. Freedom comes through enlightenment, and that enlightenment comes through opening our consciousness to that which cannot be seen, heard, tasted, touched, or smelled, to a Power invisible, a Power that does not war with other powers, but dissolves everything that appears in the nature of an enemy—whether without our being or within.

The enlightenment that sets us free consists first of all in knowing that there is a divine Power, equally present in every individual, regardless of his nationality, race, or religion, regardless of whether he lives in freedom or slavery, whether he is in a prison or out, in a hospital or out. Within each one of us there is this potential, this spiritual impulse, this Kingdom, this Presence and Power, which the Master revealed would set us free.

"Ye shall know the truth, and the truth shall make you free" [1]—not the sword, not a revolution, not rebellion, and not fighting people, governments, or outside prison-keepers, but quietly and gently realizing that slavery and limitation are

[1] John 8:32.

within ourselves, the result of our ignorance of true being, and that the remedy, therefore, must also be within us.

Only one thing has to do with our slavery, and that is ignorance. Being ignorant does not mean being uneducated or without formal schooling. Ignorance in this context always means an ignorance of truth, for it is the truth that will make us free. Admitting then that our ignorance of truth is holding us in bondage to the body and its ills and to economic or political limitation, there must be a willingness on our part to withdraw condemnation from the external world and to acknowledge that in proportion as we overcome spiritual ignorance within ourselves and attain a measure of spiritual light will freedom come into our experience.

In a great measure we may be able to live as having dominion over our body, and even if we do not seem to accomplish that in its fullness and completeness at this particular time, let that not concern us because if we can demonstrate 80 to 90 per cent of freedom from those things that are troubling the world, we will have attained a high measure of harmony in life while still tabernacling here on earth. We may experience freedom only in an infinitesimal degree tomorrow or the day after, but even if progress is gradual it is certain, and as time passes and we remain true to the spiritual principles that we learn and apply, more and more freedom is realized.

Even though there remains a measure of darkness and spiritual ignorance which must be overcome, if there is some recognition that there is a potential of freedom within us, and if there is a recognition that our troubles are not because of someone or some circumstance external to us but rather through this inner ignorance, then we are opening the way for our own freedom to begin to appear.

Regardless of how far we go on the Path, we can never expect to exercise a freedom external to ourselves, for the Christ, that which overcometh, is an overcomer of our self and establishes freedom within our consciousness which then becomes externalized by the power of truth.

Real freedom can be attained only by virtue of the recognition of the Christ within us, and by learning to live, not only in subjection to It, but in the realization of Its dominion over the circumstances and conditions of life itself. It was planted in the midst of us for that purpose. "Son, thou art ever with me, and all that I have is thine" [2] —but until we acknowledge Him in all our ways, we will not come under His government.

GOD CONSTITUTES INDIVIDUAL BEING

Only through understanding that God, the infinite Love of this universe, is expressing Itself as individual being, can we release God from responsibility for the bondage in which this world is held, and then take the next step of releasing man. God is forever expressing Itself as the fulfillment of Its own being, and God appears as the life of man, woman, child, animal, vegetable, and mineral, regardless of how false a material concept we may entertain of that life. Because of the infinite nature of God, there can be only one Life, and that Life is God expressing Itself as Life in, and as, infinite form and variety.

With this as a basic principle, whenever any kind of an erroneous picture presents itself, whether in the form of a person, a condition of health, supply, employment, or of human relationships, instantly we realize:

> *God expresses Itself as individual being. Regardless of the appearance or of the degree of mortality that is presenting itself to my eyes and ears—whether it is the criminal, the insane, the dying, or the dead—regardless of all appearances, God alone is, and God alone is the entity and identity of all being.*

[2] Luke 15:31.

God constitutes individual being. God is the life, the Soul, the Spirit, and the mind of individual being; God is the law unto individual being. Èven the body is the temple of God.

God constitutes individual being, and therefore the nature of individual being is godly and good, and in it there is nothing that "defileth . . . or maketh a lie." [3]

Whether at this moment that being is appearing as a friend, a prisoner in a prison, a sick person in a hospital or in a mental institution, regardless of what the appearance may be, the basic point is that God constitutes individual being. God alone appears as individual being in whom there is no fault.

EVIL IS IMPERSONAL

With the acceptance of the premise that God appears as individual being, and with that as the basic principle, it is useless to try to find the cause of the error in a person or to attempt to uncover the wrong thinking that produced the error. Can there be any wrong thinking in God appearing as individual being, in a being constituted of the nature, character, and quality of God?

Often when we are dealing with our friends, our relatives, our students, or our patients, we are prone to revert to a human sense of criticism and judgment or to the metaphysical sense of believing that there is something in their minds—perhaps their wrong thinking—that has to be corrected. That is true, but not true as generally understood. It is not their wrong thinking about a person, thing, or condition that needs to be corrected. The only thing that has to be corrected is the same thing that has to be corrected in all of us: the belief in two powers, the belief that God is not omnipotent, that God is not omniscient and omnipresent.

[3] Revelation 21:27.

The whole theory of resentment causing rheumatism, jealousy causing cancer, or sensuality causing tuberculosis is nonsense—pure nonsense. Those who accept a psychosomatic cause for disease find that they do not know how to get rid of the negative qualities of human thought to which all of us are heir, even after they have diagnosed this negativism as cause. The only way to be rid of these undesirable qualities is through understanding that they are not personal: they are impersonal; they are not power; they have no law to sustain them.

Ulcers are not caused by worry, and cancer is not caused by hate or jealousy, or rheumatism by resentment. The truth is that error is not personal, and it does not have its beginning in you or in me or in any other person. But if we do not understand the nature of error before it touches us, we may spend the remainder of our lives tilting at windmills and trying to fight something that is not there. *Evil is not personal: it is impersonal*. You and I are not evil. It is true that we may hate, we may fear, we may commit adultery, we may even murder; but it is not you or I doing this because the truth is that Christ is our true identity.

Then what about the appearance: the appearance of evil, the appearance of sin, disease, lack, limitation, unemployment, a nasty disposition, miserliness, or profligacy? What of it? It is impersonal, and the very moment that we understand and declare it to be impersonal, we begin to separate it from ourselves. We take the condemnation from off our own shoulders, much as the Master did when he said to the woman taken in adultery, "Neither do I condemn thee: go, and sin no more." [4] How her face must have lighted! Can you imagine the condemnation in which she was holding herself by believing that she was an adulteress, a sinner, and a criminal? But here was a man, the greatest spiritual light of the ages, saying to her, "Neither do I condemn thee."

[4] John 8:11.

This truth I myself have felt when human nature would have its way with me, and I have been aware of my own human errors. It has helped immeasurably for me to realize, "Wait a minute, wait a minute—no condemnation, no self-condemnation! Remember your true identity. Remember that this that is troubling you is of the earth earthy. It was here before you were born, and it probably will afflict others not yet born—unless their parents know enough to bring them into this world as spiritual beings and never hold them in condemnation."

There is no such thing as personal evil, nor is there such a thing as evil for which you and I individually are responsible. We are not responsible for any of the sins, diseases, lacks, or limitations that come into our experience. It is not our wrong thinking that has produced them; it is not our envy, jealousy, or malice that has produced them; it is not our greed, lust, or our mad ambition. These errors are not due to any fault that is to be found in us because in reality we are not responsible for the evils which express themselves in, as, or through us.

This sounds very comforting for the moment. It becomes disturbing only when I carry this to its logical conclusion and tell you that neither is your wife nor your husband responsible for any of these evils. The truth about you is that you, in your true identity, are the child of God. God has expressed Itself on earth individually as you. The life which is God is your individual life, and it is eternal and immortal. Your mind is actually that same mind which was in Christ Jesus, infinitely wise, infinitely pure. Your Soul is spotless, and there is not anything that you could do that would change that because God is your Soul. God is your very being, and even your body is the temple of the living God. This is the truth about you and your life, your mind, your Soul, your body, and your being.

God constitutes the identity of individual being. There is no other, and we are not going to accept any other into our consciousness. God is the only life of all being. God is the only mind. God is the only law operating and functioning. God is the only being, and besides God there is no other. When we have established this truth firmly in our consciousness, we are no longer thinking of a person as being sick or evil.

ALL PROBLEMS, A UNIVERSAL MESMERISM

But what about this case of the flu, this infection, this contagion, this epidemic? Instantly, must come the realization that evil, regardless of its name or nature, is never personal. It does not have its rise in you or in me, in him, in her, or in it. Therefore, we never have to heal a person, reform, improve, or enrich him because there is no evil in him. God constitutes his being, and only that which is God in expression is true of him. Therefore, as the son of God he is ageless, diseaseless, painless, perfect, spiritual, and incorporeal.

The appearance is not a person, not a condition, not a thing; it belongs to nobody. It is a universal mesmerism, a universal suggestion, and it operates without being seen or heard, yet it enters our consciousness.

In World War I, the citizens of the United States had no desire or inclination for war, as is evidenced by the fact that they re-elected a man to the presidency on the slogan that he had kept them out of war. Yet six months later the country was at war. This was because the suggestion of the inevitability of war was thrown out into space, and eventually, all those who had elected the President because he had kept them out of war were crying, "Let us get into this war! Let us get at the Huns!" That was no more their nature than it was your nature or mine to want to become involved in World War II. This was mesmeric suggestion imposed from without.

It is in this same way that every bit of evil of which we are a part has first been implanted in us, and much of it in such a way that we are unaware of it. Some of it, of course, is suggested to us. Many movies and some stage productions appeal directly to our senses and bring forth a sensual response, but this same response could be produced without our being consciously aware of it, and we might not understand why it was that we experienced some emotion quite foreign to us, even though we can be assured that it must have existed somewhere in consciousness.

Fear, too, enters a person's world in the morning, and he wonders why he should be afraid when there is apparently no particular reason for it. This also is a mesmeric activity or suggestion which comes into his consciousness without his ever really being aware of it. Illness, sin, and false appetites are projected in much the same way, not consciously by anybody, but through this mesmeric influence of the belief in two powers: good and evil.

BECOMING FREE OF UNIVERSAL SUGGESTION

The metaphysician and student of spiritual wisdom, however, have a way of keeping themselves free from such influences in their lives. They separate themselves from becoming statistics —those who come under the law of averages or are affected by these seen and unseen influences—and instead of blaming some person or circumstance for the discords of life, they have learned to impersonalize and realize that all evil has its source in the belief in two powers, and that it has no power of projection because it is not God-ordained or God-sustained.

Despite our desire to spare our families and our children difficult experiences, we cannot, because this truth has to be accepted in individual consciousness. To some extent, we can do this for a person for a time, but eventually the person himself, through an activity of truth in his consciousness, must separate himself from sin, disease, death, lack, limitation, or the effects of wars and depressions. He must free himself, and he must do it consciously by realizing:

"I and my Father are one," [5] *and all that the Father has is mine. Therefore, all that emanates from God expresses itself in my experience. That which is not of God, the impersonal evil, is not maintained or sustained by God and has no person in, on, as, or through whom to operate.*

Thus he frees himself.

This is a universal principle, but those who are not open, receptive, and responsive to it do not benefit from it. It is for this reason that this principle is most effective in our own experience, and often in that of those who are close to us. Teachers of spiritual wisdom also become a law of harmony to their students, but this may not continue if their students become leaners and expect the teacher to keep them out of trouble forever.

We cannot separate ourselves from sin, sinful desires, false appetites, or accidents except through a conscious activity of our own consciousness, and this activity must be a specific one:

I am under the spiritual law of God, not material or mental laws. I am not subject to such laws because in my alignment with spiritual entity, only spiritual law can act in me, on me, and through me.

"AN ARM OF FLESH"

This whole principle of the nothingness of temporal power and material law is exemplified by the response of Hezekiah when his people came to him beset by fear because the enemy was about to attack them and they were outnumbered greatly:

[5] John 10:30.

"With him is an arm of flesh; but with us is the Lord our God to help us." [6] He did not deny that the enemy had men, equipment, and weapons; he merely said that they had temporal weapons, temporal arms, "an arm of flesh."

Today we have discovered that all the evils of the world represent the "arm of flesh," or temporal power, which in the presence of God is not power. This is not using truth over error or calling upon God to do something to evil. It is not acknowledging a great power which will do something to other powers. No, this is standing foursquare on the truth that God is the only power. All else, whether it is called material power or mental power, is temporal power, impersonal nothingness.

This was the strength David had when he stood before Goliath. This was the strength of Jesus Christ as he stood before Pilate: "Thou couldest have no power at all against me, except it were given thee from above." [7]

And what about the crippled, the blind, the sinning, the poor? Did Jesus turn to God and beseech Him to heal them, to forgive or enrich them? Or did he say: "Arise, take up thy bed.[8] . . . Be thou clean.[9] . . . Thy sins be forgiven thee.[10] . . . All that I have is thine." [11] In other words, what power is there other than God-power? Jesus' entire teaching is "resist not evil." [12]

Why should we not resist evil? Because evil is not power. It is only a suggestion or a temptation, which we do not have to accept. It comes to us as a suggestion of good or evil, health or sickness; it comes to us as a suggestion of a power, but we do

[6] II Chronicles 32:8.
[7] John 19:11.
[8] Matthew 9:6.
[9] Matthew 8:3.
[10] Matthew 9:2.
[11] Luke 15:31.
[12] Matthew 5:39.

not have to accept it. We do not have to accept the fall of Adam and Eve, which came about because they believed in two powers, good and evil. We can revert to our spiritual self-hood and accept God as the all and all of being and then look upon material or mental forces as the "arm of flesh," or nothingness.

One thing above all we must never forget: if we ever blame a person for anything, we are setting the trap into which we ourselves will eventually fall. If we blame heads of state for our troubles, if we blame union leaders or management for our troubles, if we blame politicians or politics for them, we are setting the trap for ourselves. It is true that many of these persons are instruments for evil, but they are not the evil, and this evil cannot operate in the presence of a consciousness of one Power.

The ability to impersonalize evil comes about as the result of some measure of spiritual realization. For example, if I were to go out on a street corner and announce to the people assembled there that there are no thieves, no immoral or bad people, can you imagine what would happen? They would be listening with the mind, without any developed spiritual sense, and would have no understanding of what was being said; whereas, when I tell you that there never has been an evil person in the world and there never will be, you understand what is meant. There are times, however, when we and everybody else are the instruments through which evil manifests, but that does not make us evil. It merely testifies to our ignorance of how to protect ourselves from the mesmeric influence of world beliefs.

Every spiritual principle that is ever voiced is utter nonsense to the human mind. But by the time you have arrived at the state of consciousness that would lead you to read this book, you must have developed a measure of spiritual consciousness and should be able to understand the impersonal nature of evil, an understanding of which takes a degree of spiritual illumination.

Let us understand clearly the universal, impersonal nature of evil. Both good and evil are floating around in space just as radio or television broadcasts are in the ether, and therefore any place can be a mass of either good or evil suggestions. Subconsciously, we are tuned in to these suggestions, and some of them have an effect upon us. To become free of any mesmeric influence that may be operating in any place, it is necessary for us to know:

> Only that which emanates from the divine Source can find inlet and outlet through me. I and my Father, the creative principle of Life, are one. All the mesmeric beliefs of good and evil—whatever their name or nature—have no inlet or outlet because they are of this one source, the nothingness of an impersonal universal belief.

Across the Desk

It is just a few hours before Christmas 1963, and I have been sitting here all week opening several thousand envelopes containing the love and gratitude of students from all six continents and many of the islands on earth. Of course, you cannot possibly imagine my feelings as I open these envelopes filled with heartwarming messages, gifts, contributions to the activities, personal gifts to Emma and to me, and I realize that all this is an outpouring of the Spirit to God, not to man.

None of this would really be coming to me for myself, and every bit of it is sent to me only as a representative of the infinite Invisible, or as a transparency for God. All this is an outpouring of the Soul of man to God. It is an acknowledgment of the omnipresence of God and a recognition of God manifest as man on earth, not as a mortal, but as Man himself, the real Man, the real Self hidden within each individual.

It is a joy to witness an outpouring of this nature, and then to realize that many of these messages represent the love of two, three, or four in a household, and in some cases, entire groups in cities of the United States and Canada, of Australia, New Zealand, and South Africa, of the United Kingdom, Sweden, Holland, Germany, and Switzerland, and to realize that there are these thousands lifting their thoughts and expressing their love toward God and recognizing His grace on earth.

Looking out of the eyes at the visible scene, one sees much of man's inhumanity to man, even in this latter half of the twentieth century, and much misunderstanding, not only between different nations and races, but misunderstanding among the people within each country. If one were to judge by this, the human scene would be sad to witness, but I ask you now to see through my eyes and to witness what I have witnessed here all month in the opening of this mail, and rejoice that you are one of those thousands upon thousands who are united in consciousness in an actual Christmas Season of adoration, of love, and of gratitude to the one Spirit that you are recognizing as indwelling the Soul and consciousness of every individual.

Still looking out through my eyes, behold all mankind everywhere, even in the deepest sense of ignorance of his true identity, and remember that there, too, lies the unawakened Soul, awaiting only your recognition to cause it to spring into an awakening.

As I have opened each envelope and each package since the second day that the mail started pouring in this month, this has been my conscious thought: "Here, God, is a gift to You from another Soul recognizing Omnipresence, Omnipotence, and

Omniscience. May this greeting and this gift pass through me to Thee, and may Thy grace fall upon each one who has sent this message through me to You, and may all of these gifts be dedicated to Your service and be returned by You, not only to the givers, but to all those for whom these gifts were meant." In this way, I have given recognition to the fact that in thanking, honoring, and in greeting me, you were actually doing all this unto God through me, and be assured that I have let your gifts and your greetings flow through me to the throne of God, there to be blessed and returned to earth.

May I give you this gift this year? With every gift or contribution that you make to any spiritual activity, and with every dollar that you spend for spiritual or philanthropic purposes, will you please remember that you are giving your gift to God through those individuals who will seemingly benefit.

In Freemasonry, one of the major activities is benevolence in different forms. There are medical bodies which they sponsor, devoting their lives to research to overcome the universal belief of old age; there are hospitals for crippled children open to children of any race or religion whose families cannot afford to pay for such help; there are homes for the aged; and there is relief for widows or orphans, and many other activities of a philanthropic nature. All these are for the purpose of teaching members of the Fraternity the joy and the blessings of giving and sharing.

To me, it has always been clear that this is not so much for the benefit of the poor as it is a benefit, a blessing, and a lesson to those who give, revealing to those who have eyes and those who have ears that the giving is always in conformity with the Master's teaching as given in Matthew: "Inasmuch as ye have done it unto one of the least of these my brethren, ye have done it unto me." [13] and in the same way, never forget that "inas-

[13] Matthew 25:40.

much as ye did it not to one of the least of these, you did it not to me." [14] Let my gift to you be the remembrance that in giving to any spiritual or philanthropic cause, you must at all times remember that you are giving unto God through man.

[14] Matthew 25:45.

3) "Get Thee Hence, Satan"

It took a really great mystic to discover the secret of impersonal evil and devise the name "devil" or "Satan" for it. This devil or Satan, as it was first conceived, did not mean an opponent of God; it had no such meaning at all. Instead, it meant something in the nature of a tempter—not a power or a person, but a tempter offering temptation. The evil is never in us; it is the tempter that tempts us into sin, disease, death, lack, and limitation, and this tempter should be recognized at all times as the impersonal source of evil.

When the devil stood before Jesus in the wilderness tempting him to turn the stones into bread, Jesus answered, "Man shall not live by bread alone, but by every word that proceedeth out of the mouth of God." [1] Again Satan tempted the Master to cast himself down from the pinnacle of the temple, and

[1] Matthew 4:4.

Jesus' answer was, "Thou shalt not tempt the Lord thy God." [2] Once more Satan offered him temptation in the form of worldly glory, and to this, Jesus replied, "Get thee hence, Satan." [3] With this recognition of the devil as the impersonal source of evil, Satan left him.

From then on what do we hear about Satan as far as the Master is concerned? He does not appear any more. He seems to have faded out, right there and then. With that "Get thee hence, Satan," Satan is no more. The Master is alone, alone with God, consciously one with God, the victor, with full dominion. But the tempter, the devil, is gone; the temptation is gone.

TEMPTATION ALWAYS APPEARS AS A PERSON OR A CONDITION

Every need for help for yourself or any call for help that comes from someone else should be recognized as a temptation, a temptation to be rejected. Even if it should be someone close to a hundred years, suffering from old age, remember that the claim of age has to do merely with the calendar. The calendar affects us only if we accept it, keep looking at it every day, and wondering what story it tells, instead of proving how impersonal it can be by commanding it to "get thee behind me, Satan."

Temptation will always come in the form of a person, a disease, a sin, or a lack. It will not come in the form of a man with a cloven hoof, or in the form of anyone or anything that can be identified. Often it comes in the guise of good, and we must be alert to recognize that sometimes good is as much of an evil as evil itself. Once we have learned to impersonalize every phase of good as well as of evil, however, we will not be

2 Matthew 4:7.
3 Matthew 4:10.

fooled so easily, nor will we ever look at any person in an attempt to see what is in him that might be causing his difficulty.

Error has its rise in an impersonal source which in the beginning was called eating of the fruit "of the tree of the knowledge of good and evil." [4] Anyone can begin to demonstrate harmony in his experience in proportion to his giving up the temptation to talk about one thing as good and another as evil, and in proportion to his realization that in a God-created universe there can be neither good nor evil: there can be only God, Spirit.

The biggest temptation that will ever come to us is to believe that one person is good and another evil, whereas no one is good and no one is evil. No human being, in his humanhood, can ever truthfully say that he is spiritual. To claim spirituality as a personal possession is egotism at its height. No one is spiritual; no one is perfect; and no one is evil: God is Spirit and only God is perfect; and evil is impersonal error.

THE BELIEF IN TWO POWERS IS THE TEMPTATION

When it was revealed that man personally is not a sinner, but that there is a tempter called devil, or Satan, in some way this devil or Satan became known as, and understood to be, the opposite of God, the opponent of God, an enemy of God, something that God had to fight and get rid of. But be assured of this—and I say it only through revelation—God has nothing to fight at any time, no one to fight, and nothing to overcome. God *is,* and God is omnipotence, and besides God, there is none else. God has no battles. God has no enemies. God has no opponents. The devil can walk up and down the world parading its wares, but if everybody says, "No," to the temptation offered, that will be the end of the devil, and this, without any

[4] Genesis 2:17.

help from God. We do not need God to fight the devil for us. We need only the words, "No, get thee behind me."

Paul gave us another name for the devil or evil when he called it "carnal mind," [5] although he, too, made the mistake that most modern metaphysicians have made of fighting the evil. Paul met with all manner of persecution—beatings and imprisonment—because he made the carnal mind "enmity against God." [5] Carnal mind is the "arm of flesh," [6] or nothingness. It is a tempter that can tempt us to believe in a power apart from God, but it cannot make it so any more than the devil could make Jesus succumb to those temptations. No, carnal mind is a tempter; carnal mind is a claim of two powers; carnal mind is always presenting appearances of sin, disease, death, lack, and limitation; but these are nothing more than appearances. They are not reality.

For our purpose, we use terms such as devil, carnal mind, hypnotism, or mesmerism. As a matter of fact, one of the best words to use in describing evil is the word "appearance." Just as the illusion on the desert is not a thing or an entity but an appearance, so the evils that present themselves to us are not real: they have no identity; they have no substance; and they have no law. We may therefore look upon them as appearances.

The point that I would make is this: error did not have its rise in you or in me; it did not have its rise in wrong thinking; it did not have its rise in hate, envy, or jealousy. It had its rise in the acceptance of the belief that there are two powers. No man invented it or discovered it. This universal belief, which comes to us every minute of the day and night for acceptance or rejection, this belief in good and evil, this belief in two powers, is all there is to the carnal mind.

[5] Romans 8:7.
[6] II Chronicles 32:8.

THE NOTHINGNESS AND NONPOWER OF TEMPTATION

Is it consistent to declare God to be infinite and all power, and then in the same breath ascribe power to something else, giving it the power to cause disease, sin, or lack? If we are to love God supremely, it can only be because we accept God as the only power there is. How can anyone love a God that not only is not the only power, but is not even strong enough to take care of the devil in all these thousands of years? I do not believe that it is possible for anyone to love God with all his heart and soul while at the same time he believes in two powers, regardless of how much he may mouth his love of God. One can love God only in the realization of the supreme nature of God's being, and that makes evil of no power.

In understanding God as being the only and all-power, having nothing with which to contend—no one and no condition —abiding in the supreme infinite nature of God's being, and then recognizing all these appearances as the "arm of flesh," or a temptation to believe in two powers, evil conditions will disappear and evaporate. They will come back, however, if we fasten the evil onto a person, that is, if we personalize. "Sin no more, lest a worse thing come unto thee." [7]

When we fight the devil, or carnal mind, we set up our own enemy, build it in our mind, and authorize it to stay there until something else gets rid of it. We have put it there, built it, called it carnal or mortal mind, and then given it evil propensities. Had we accepted God as Omnipotence, we would have said, "Carnal mind? Mortal mind? What of it? It must be that arm of flesh the Hebrew prophet was talking about that we do not have to war against. What we have to do is to rest in the Word."

We rest in the word that the carnal mind is not enmity against God. It is the "arm of flesh," a nothingness which

7 John 5:14.

must be understood to be an impersonal source of evil, impersonal, meaning without a person, without a you or a me. We are the person it is without—*when we impersonalize it.*

Devil, carnal mind, or mortal mind? It has only the power that universal belief gives it, and that is why we suffer from it without even knowing that it exists. But once we awaken, once we understand that the devil, Satan, mortal mind, or carnal mind is not power, but is a suggestion offering itself to us for acceptance, we can say, "No," and then forget it.

Devil, carnal mind, or mortal mind has no existence. In all this world, it would be impossible to find a carnal mind, a mortal mind, or a devil. Then what is this devil, carnal mind, or mortal mind that we are talking about? It is the very thing that cast Adam and Eve out of the Garden: a belief in two powers. When we believe in two powers, we have a mortal mind or a carnal mind, and it can tear us to pieces; but we are free of it in proportion as we understand that God never made a power to destroy God or God's creation. God is the only creative principle of this universe, for God is omnipotence, omniscience, omnipresence, and therefore, there is no power of evil.

STOP BATTLING ERROR

Strange how, throughout the ages, religious men and women have dedicated their lives to the one purpose of overcoming the devil, and the devil has no power! The devil is nothing except what we decide to make it. The metaphysical world has made the self-same mistake. It will tell you that there is no devil or Satan: there is just mortal mind. Nevertheless, all kinds of quotations and affirmations are concocted to overcome this mortal mind, and thereby many sincere truth-students take a beating because of their belief in mortal mind.

All there is to what is called mortal mind is the belief in

good and evil. There is no such thing as mortal mind as an entity; there is no such thing as carnal mind as an entity; there is no such thing as devil or Satan as an entity: there is only a universal belief in two powers, and that belief is the cause of every bit of discord and inharmony that has ever existed on the face of the earth.

In the degree that we fight or battle this so-called carnal mind or any of its individual forms and expressions, in that degree will we lose because we have created an enemy greater than ourselves, one with which God cannot help us because God has no knowledge of it. God is too pure to behold iniquity.

It was not the teaching of Jesus Christ to pray to God, "Please overcome my enemies! Please destroy my enemies! Please go out before me and slay these terrible people!" That is a superstitious and ignorant form of prayer, but certainly not enlightened Christian prayer. The overcoming has to be within us, and the overcoming that has to take place within us is our recognition of the truth:

I *will never leave you, nor forsake you. If you go through the waters, you will not drown, and if you go through the fire, the flames will not kindle upon you.*

Why? Because they have no such power.

As we realize this, we shall understand why Jesus could forgive the woman taken in adultery, the thief on the cross, and Judas who betrayed him. He knew through divine revelation that these had no power.

"Destroy this temple, and in three days I will raise it up. . . . But he spake of the temple of his body." [8] This applies also to the body of our affairs, the body of our relationships, of our home, our work, and our supply. Certainly, depressions may

8 John 2:19, 21.

come and deprive us of our savings, our wealth, and our investments, but they are only the body of supply: they are not supply. God is our supply, and if we lose what we consider to be the body of our supply, we can begin at once to build it again. There is no limit. There is no such thing as having only one chance, or even two or three. The only question is how much we ourselves are able to accept spiritual principles and then how much we practice them until they become a living force within our own being.

THERE IS NO POWER
IN THE DISCORDS OF THIS WORLD

I understand, of course, how difficult it is to look at the sins, diseases, and horrors of the world and not believe that there is power in them. It is possible to do this only after you feel within you a certain rightness about these principles and then are willing to put them into practice until such time as you witness the first healing as a result of the application of them.

The first time that anyone is healed through your realization that you have not appealed to God and have not expected truth to remove error, but have rested in the realization that there is only one power and that nothing has any power except what comes from above, you will know that you have witnessed these principles in action. Then you will have the courage to go on and on until you are able to do some of the greater works, because you have watched the enemy destroy itself; you have seen the appearances destroy themselves.

If God made all that was made and all that God made is good, then God did not make a carnal mind, a mortal mind, a devil, or a Satan, and it, therefore, has no existence except as a mental concept in human thought. If you would like to demonstrate how powerless a human concept is, close your eyes and build the biggest bomb you can possibly build. Build an atomic bomb and combine it with hydrogen and with all the forms of nuclear fission you have ever heard about, multiply it by a thousand, then throw it, and see how powerless it is to do anything. It is only a mental concept, and a mental concept has no substance; it has no law; it has no entity; it has no being. True, it has form, and that is why you can see it, but you can see it only in your mind as a mental image.

Once you begin to understand that the devil is a man-made entity formed in the mind of man, not in the mind of God, and that it has no law, no substance, no activity, no source, no avenue, and no channel, you nullify it. You have recognized it for what it is: temporal power, the "arm of flesh," nothingness.

It is with that realization that healing work begins. Actually, regardless of the name or nature of the problem with which you are confronted, you can be assured of this: it is nothing but a temptation of the devil coming to you for acceptance or rejection. This devil is nothing more nor less than the carnal mind, the human mind, which exists because of a belief in good and evil. When there is no belief in good and evil, there is no human mind any more, no carnal mind. You are then operating in, and through, and with the mind of God. It is only as long as there is a belief in good and evil that there is limitation, finiteness, negativeness.

The reason that healing is possible is because God is, and God constitutes this universe. God constitutes your being and mine, and that being is perfect. But because of a sense of separation we are mesmerized by the belief in two powers, and without our consciously knowing it, it becomes a part of our consciousness, and we respond to it in the same way that we do to the subliminal advertising that is thrown into the unconscious or subconscious.[9]

[9] For a complete discussion of this subject, see the author's *The Art of Spiritual Healing* (New York: Harper and Row, 1959) pp. 61, 62.

ERROR, A MESMERIC SENSE OF REALITY

There is a God maintaining and sustaining the integrity of this universe, and it is perfect except when we see it "through a glass, darkly," [10] except when we see it through a sense that has been to some extent mesmerized by the belief in good and evil. The healing lies in our realization that God's universe is intact, and therefore we are intact, for all that God is we are, and all that the Father has is ours. This that is appearing is just the product of mesmeric sense, but since it is not God-created, God-ordained, or God-sustained, it is a nothingness, the "arm of flesh."

As we abide in this truth of the unreal nature of evil, it begins to dissolve before our very eyes, because it does not exist as a person and it does not exist as a condition. It exists as a mesmeric influence, owing to our acceptance of the belief in two powers as real.

A person is not evil even if he appears as the most ruthless and tyrannical dictator the world has ever known. He will be evil to us if we see him as evil, but he cannot be that to us if we see him as he is in his true identity and realize that the evil we are beholding is not an evil person: it is a mesmeric influence which is being accepted as reality. That is the secret. If we do not accept it as reality, it cannot operate against us.

As we sow, so shall we reap. If we believe that there is a sinful man, then sin can be committed against us. If we believe that there is a poverty-stricken man, poverty can knock at our door. If we believe that there is disease and death, we can experience them. *In the kingdom of God,* no man, woman, or child has ever died. There has never been a death since time began *in the kingdom of God*—never one. Passing from sight is part of the mesmeric influence. Those who are born must die; those who believe in birth must believe in death, for they are those

[10] I Corinthians 13:12.

who have not been able to see that this human picture is really immortal, eternal, and spiritual, but that it is seen falsely through the belief in two powers.

The beginning of wisdom is to know that God is, that God constitutes and is the substance of all that is, the life, the activity, and the law of all that is, and therefore this is an immortal and eternal universe, and we are eternal and immortal beings. Then that which we behold as a limited finite world, as evil in any form—sin, disease, lack, limitation, war, depressions, storms—we must understand to be the product of a universal mesmeric sense, that which was originally called devil but is now called carnal mind, or mortal mind. Because it never was of God, but was formed in the mind of man after the Fall of Man and his acceptance of two powers, it exists only as a mental picture, without power and without continuity. It thereby begins to fade and fade until it is no more.

Healing work is accomplished on that basis, but it is not accomplished by praying to God for help, by praying to God for employment, supply, activity, or any other kind of a gift. It is accomplished by realizing that the mind of God is actually our very mind, that all the capacities of that God-mind are our capacities, and that the picture that confronts us is a mesmeric picture, forever without law.

Healings take place, not because God has done us a favor and not because we have found some person we think is closer to God than we are. That is all nonsense. There is no one closer to God than we are. There are just those who have learned the nature and the origin of sin and disease and, thereby, know how to dissolve them.

If disease, sin, or any earthly condition were really a fact, a truth, or a being, God would have to be responsible for it, and the nature of it would be good instead of evil. It is not possible for God to be divided against Himself. It is not possible for an infinite Intelligence to act destructively against Itself or Its own creation. Therefore, we can accept the fact that God is perfection itself, and all that God has done and has made is good, and anything that God did not do or make does not exist. Neither sin, disease, death, storms, nor anything like that was ever made by God. They appear to us because of a universal belief in two powers, and our realization of that is the healing agency. Our realization of the nothingness of that which is frightening and confronting us as evil is the very presence and power that dissolves it, and nothing else will do it.

BREAKING THE MESMERISM

When we are faced with discords, inharmonies, unhappiness, lacks, and limitation, let us not go to God to try to get God to change these discords. Let us turn away from these, look right out into the world, and realize:

> *This is but a part of the universal mesmerism, trying to convince me that God is not on the field, that God is not my life and being, trying to convince me there are two powers on earth. But I know better. I know that there cannot be an infinite God and an evil power.*

Abiding in that word and letting that word abide in us, we break the mesmerism—not by might, not by power, but by understanding. Heaven cannot be taken by storm. We cannot gain heaven by might or by power, but only by an inner, silent, sacred communion, and that not for any purpose except for the joy of communing. When there is anything interfering with our well-being or that of someone who is looking to us for help, right there God is on the field. God is always present. We do not have to urge God to act in anyone's behalf. All we have to do is face the impersonal source of all evil and recognize its nothingness, its lawlessness, and then be still and watch—

watch the carnal mind and its pictures pass away from us. It is only necessary to reassure ourselves that God is:

> God is the substance of all form, and this world is perfect because it is God's world. If I am being faced with a picture of a dying person, a poor or sinful person, or an imprisoned one, that is the mesmeric activity of the carnal mind presenting this picture to me.
>
> How grateful I am that I have learned that there is no law in this picture to sustain it, no substance, no form, no activity, so it must dissolve!

If we constantly have in mind these major principles, we must come to a complete conviction that God is, and this means that harmony is. It means that the entire kingdom of God is at peace and at-one with God. Then we realize that the only disturbance to our peace and harmony is caused by whatever it is that has convinced us that there are two powers. When we begin to understand that this belief is the fleshly mind, the "arm of flesh," or a nothingness, that is when the pictures of sense are dissolved.

That is why the person who does not rush out like a fireman to get his hat and coat and run to see the patient does the best work. The one who rushes to the scene will probably lose his case quickly because he has accepted the condition as a power. The mesmerism is broken by the person who can realize:

> Nothing is going on in the kingdom of God about which I need to be disturbed, and what is going on to the human sense of things is not real, has no law to support it, and no power or continuity.

In the silent contemplation of this truth, the mesmerism is broken, and along with it the picture disappears. That is how healing work is accomplished.

In our own being, let us be sure that we are not looking to God for something, that we have given up all thought or belief that we are going to get something from God that God is not already giving us. Rather let us understand that all that God is, is flowing now. All that God has is pouring forth now. God is. God is the same yesterday, today, and forevermore, so let us not annoy God! God is.

All the evils of this world are nothing but pictures in the mind, and when we know this they begin to dissolve. They begin to dissolve the very minute we know the nature of error. All evil functions as the universal carnal mind, the universal mesmeric mind, but since it is not law and has no law, since it is not being, since God did not ordain it, since God does not maintain it or sustain it, we do not fear it, nor do we fight it. We resist not evil. We put up our sword. We are at peace. God is.

HEALING COMES THROUGH A REALIZATION OF THE
PRINCIPLES OF IMPERSONALIZATION AND
"NOTHINGIZATION"

Your healings will be miraculous, but only in proportion to your ability to impersonalize and "nothingize." It is not your patient who is responsible for his ills, nor is it anybody else. It is not your patient who is responsible for his nature or his character—or lack of it. It is only his ignorance of how to separate himself from these impersonal or devilish influences which come to him as temptations or suggestions but which, in and of themselves, are nothing until he accepts or believes them.

Spiritual healing has its foundation in God, but it is not a going to God for the healing, nor expecting God to do anything. It has its foundation in the realization that God never gives and God never withholds: God is forever being, harmonious being. Then follows your recognition of the fact that everything and anything of a nature unlike God belongs in the category of devil, Satan, or carnal mind, which is temporal power, nothingness.

In actual practice, you will come up against specific conditions such as infection and contagion which you will have to learn to handle in this impersonal way. Always, there are epidemics of one kind or another, and you will have to learn that these are not conditions of matter, nor are they conditions of weather: these are projections of the carnal mind, having no power.

The moment you try to deal with infection or contagion, you will fail because you will be on the *materia medica* level which operates from the standpoint of the power of germs, infection, and contagion. But you cannot do this. You can work only from the spiritual level, and that level knows the nothingness of what appears as destructive germs. We do not deny germs. I suppose in our human experience we could not live without them. What we do deny is the destructive nature of germs because God never empowered anything of a destructive nature to destroy His own creation.

You will also come up against hereditary diseases and beliefs. These must be dealt with in the same way. We were not born of the flesh. God is our only father; God is our only mother. That which is called human birth is not creation. Creation begins in the Invisible; it has its origin in God because God is the creative principle of all life, and therefore God is the only parent, and it is only from God that individual qualities can flow.

Then what of these evil qualities? They belong to that carnal mind which is no mind. Recognizing them as the carnal mind, they are thereby nullified. As long as you plant them in a man, as long as you blame them on his mother or his father, you are personalizing. You have to remove the belief in traits inherited from the parents and the grandparents and the great-grandparents. You have to stop believing that this person is this way owing to certain nationalistic, racial, or religious traits, because these traits all stem from the same source. They emanate from the carnal mind; and because their substance is the carnal mind, they are not power, they are not presence, they are not substance, they are not law.

Some of the evils you encounter will appear to you as forms that you may not recognize for what they are, and you may forget that these, too, have to be relegated to the carnal mind where they can be "nothingized."

In my thirty years of healing work, I have had the same problems to meet as every other practitioner. I have found, and you may have found this, too, that there are certain diseases that do not readily yield. However, not a single case that is called incurable really is incurable.

There is nothing impossible once you understand the nature of God and truly know the nature of error as an impersonal nothingness. But you have to be willing to stand with that principle until you can demonstrate it. Again, remember it is not because evil is nothing that it can be nullified. It is only in proportion as you can attain the consciousness of its nothingness that you can prove its nonpower. If the nothingness of evil could remove it, it would have been removed by now because it is nothing. But its nothingness will not remove it. It takes the enlightened consciousness of an individual. It takes the dedicated spiritual consciousness of an individual, and that is why there are so few healers in this age capable of doing the greater works. Anyone could do them if he would dedicate his life to this work, if he could drop other responsibilities and dedicate himself to study and to meditation until his spiritual nature so evolves that evil would automatically disappear at his approach.

There can be millions and hundreds of millions of persons who can be highly successful healers, but it is a life of dedication. The developing of the healing consciousness cannot be done in one's spare time. Yes, of course, the healing of colds, flu, or a little minor thing—that can be done. But in order to become a part of a world healing ministry and open up the rest of this world to the vision of living in God, there must arise out of society a group of persons who so want God and so want to bring God's government on earth that they dedicate themselves to this goal day and night.

Across the Desk

You will notice that each month The Infinite Way is now being given more and more recognition by the religious and educational worlds and, because of this, inevitably, you are going to be called upon to explain what The Infinite Way contribution is to the world.

To you, therefore, it must be clear that The Infinite Way reveals that:

1. There is a transcendental consciousness available to man here and now, which, when attained, results in the "dying daily" of the old man and the rebirth of the new man, the son of God. This transcendental or spiritual consciousness is the power of Grace in the experience of man, freeing him from the "law" and establishing his life under Grace.

2. There are principles of life whereby this higher consciousness is attained.

3. Through the spiritual discernment now possible, the nature of God as individual consciousness is revealed, the kingdom of God, and the secret of spiritual power.

If all this is not clear to you, begin at once a serious study of *The Contemplative Life*[11] and of the following chapters in *A Parenthesis in Eternity*[12]: "Reality and Illusion," "The Nature of Spiritual Power," and "Living Above the Pairs of Opposites."

You cannot spend all your life *taking in*, but must rather expect to be called upon to *give out*, and you cannot give out more than you understand. What you understand of The Infinite Way is the measure of your demonstration of spiritual harmony. "Freely ye have received, freely give." [13]

[11] By the author. (New York, New York: The Julian Press, 1963).
[12] By the author. (New York, New York: Harper and Row, 1963).
[13] Matthew 10:8.

4) *No* And!

The secret of meeting error lies in knowing its nature. And the nature of error can be summed up in such words as "carnal mind," "suggestion," "appearance," or "hypnotism." The nature of error as hypnotism, or the carnal mind, can be illustrated in this way: If there were a plant in the room where you are now sitting and if someone hypnotized you, he could make you believe that, instead of branches, snakes were growing out of the flowerpot, and you would accept and believe it. Through hypnotic suggestion, the hypnotist has taken temporary control of your mind, and because you are apparently unable to act independently, you follow his suggestion to its logical conclusion. A fear of the snakes is set up in you; you run away from them and may even pick up a knife with which to chop off their heads—all this based on the belief that snakes are actually there.

No matter what you might do to those nonexistent snakes,

you still could not change the fact that as long as you remain hypnotized you will see snakes. There is no possible way for you to be rid of those snakes except to become dehypnotized; there is no way to get rid of your fear of snakes except to become dehypnotized; there is no way to put up your sword except to become dehypnotized. In other words, as long as the hypnosis lasts, all the component parts of the picture are there, are they not?

Now just as it is possible to hypnotize you into believing that there are snakes in the room, so is it possible to hypnotize you into believing that there is a selfhood other than God in any place where you happen to be. As soon as you have been hypnotized into believing in a selfhood apart from God, you then logically accept all the beliefs regarding this selfhood: birth, growth, maturity, and ultimately death. There is only one way to be rid of the human picture, and that is to understand that there is no person and there is no selfhood other than God in the room or in any other place. But the hypnotized person will at once counter with, "How can you say that there is only God in the room?" And the answer is simple: there is only one Life, and that Life is God; there is only one Soul, and that Soul is God; there is only one Spirit; there is only one Law; there is only one creative Principle: God. What then can be present except God? Nothing!

The moment you see God *and,* you are hypnotized. The moment you see a mortal, material world, you are hypnotized; and from then on, there is no possible way to get rid of the appearance. That is the reason that even if you kill the snake over there in the flowerpot, two more will rise up to take its place. That is why with all the advances made in *materia medica* everybody still dies because everybody who is born must die. They do and they will. At best they may live a few more years, but that is all. People still die of pneumonia; people still die of tuberculosis; they still die of cancer; they still die of heart failure, and were a cure found for these something else would immediately replace them.

If you can agree that there is God, which means that you accept an infinite power of good, certainly then you must be able to understand that there cannot be error, disease, or death. In fact, not since time began has there ever been a single death *in the kingdom of God*.

So whatever you see in the nature of sin, disease, or death is a part of the hypnosis, and, furthermore, whatever you see as good humanhood is also a part of the same hypnosis. Even the healthy human being of thirty or forty will some day be an old human being of seventy or eighty. When you see a young, healthy person, therefore, you are just being fooled by an appearance of good. Until you can become dehypnotized to the degree that you know that there are not good human beings or bad human beings, that there are not diseased human beings or healthy human beings, but that there is only God, the one Life, the one Soul, the one Spirit, the one Substance, the one Law, the one Activity—until that time, you will have to experience death.

JUDGE NOT AFTER APPEARANCES

No one can ever be dehypnotized as long as he is judging by appearances because the human mind with which he is judging is a state of hypnotism. In other words, in looking out from our eyes, we are looking out from a state of hypnosis in which our eyes are always going to see babies being born and old people dying; our ears are always going to be hearing about sin, disease, death, lack, and limitation. Until we are able to shut off those five senses and develop an inner discernment, we are always going to see, hear, taste, touch, and smell error.

If we look through our eyes at the people of this world, all we shall ever see are human beings, sometimes good, sometimes bad. The man and wife who love each other one day drive daggers into each other's hearts the next day. The parent who fondles the child one day reproaches him the next. It is the human picture, sometimes good, sometimes evil. That is what we shall always see, hear, taste, touch, and smell with the five physical senses.

The only way to be dehypnotized is to quiet the physical senses, to be still inside, and then spiritual awareness reveals the truth of being that enables us to see that which is not visible, to hear that which is not audible, to know that which is not knowable with the human senses.

A person with no musical appreciation listening to a symphony hears only a mass of dull monotonous noises, but a person with a developed musical consciousness listening to the same symphony hears harmony, melody, and rhythm. What does a person who has no art appreciation see when he looks at a beautiful painting? Daubs of paint! That is all—nothing more, nothing less—just daubs of paint that do not make sense. On the other hand, a person with an appreciation of art sees whatever it is that the artist had in mind, and appreciates the technique, execution, coloring, and the shading.

A person who knows nothing of sculpture looks at a statue, and what does he see? A piece of bronze or marble made into a statue which to him appears only as a very poor likeness. But the person with an artistic sense looks at it, and he sees the skill expressed by the line, form, and rhythm; he sees in it the flow in the artist's mind and hands. Such people are not seeing with their eyes: they are seeing through their understanding of music and art.

And just as no one will ever be able to understand a symphony or a piece of sculpture until he develops a certain measure of artistic appreciation, so no one will ever be able to understand the spiritual universe until he develops that inner spiritual consciousness, that which is called Christ-consciousness. It was Christ-consciousness which enabled Jesus to say to Pilate, the man who had the greatest temporal power of his day in Jerusalem, "Thou couldest have no power at all against me, except it were given thee from above." [1] How could Jesus make such a daring statement in the face of the great temporal power that Pilate wielded? It was only because he had the inner vision to see through to something beyond what the eyes could see and the ears could hear. He knew something that the human being could not know, and he proved it when he allowed himself to be crucified. They could crucify him, but they could not kill him. The Crucifixion and the nails had no power.

THE DEHYPNOTIZED CONSCIOUSNESS SEES REALITY

Dehypnotism is a state of consciousness that sees that which actually is: it is the ability to see, hear, taste, touch, and smell Reality; it is the ability to see sin not as sin, and disease not as disease, but rather to be able to separate these from the person and realize that we are dealing with a *false appearance* produced by the belief in a selfhood apart from God, a universal belief so powerful that it operates as law in our consciousness until we detect and cast it out, that is, until we know the truth which makes us free.

The only way this can be accomplished is through spiritual consciousness. First of all, we must know this: we cannot cure a disease—there is none; we cannot overcome poverty—there is none; we cannot overcome death—there is none. The only thing we can do is to recognize that we are not dealing with those appearances or suggestions as such: we are dealing with hypnotism.

Even a so-called mental cause for a disease is just as much an illusion as is the physical disease. If there is a mental cause for a

1 John 19:11.

physical disease, as is claimed in some teachings, the disease is no illusion, since it has a real cause. We, in The Infinite Way, believe that even a mental cause is as much of an illusion as the physical disease, since all there is to the human scene is of the nature of illusion. The mental cause is as illusory in its nature as the physical effect.

The truth is that all there is, is infinite God and Its creation. There is nothing else. To understand Reality, we must understand that Spirit alone is real, since Spirit is infinite. All that exists, then, must exist at the standpoint of Spirit and be under spiritual law. Therefore, we are not dealing with the physical effects of mental causes: we are dealing only with God manifesting Itself and expressing Its infinite harmonies, and with the appearance, suggestion, or claim of a universal belief in a selfhood apart from God, of a universe apart from God, and of a selfhood and universe subject to material and mental laws.

THIS UNIVERSE IS GOVERNED BY PRINCIPLE

Can you believe that there is God *and* sickness, too? Where would God be while someone is suffering? Human parents would never permit a child to suffer from a disease if they could prevent it. Would you let your child suffer? Then why do you think God would? It cannot be. *In reality,* there never has been a sick person or a dead one. Everybody who has ever lived from the beginning of all time is still alive—it could not be otherwise. Unless you accept this truth, you are really an atheist and believe that the world sprang up out of dust, that it is going to return to dust, and that there is no God.

But how can you believe that when you observe the law of like begetting like in operation: apples always coming from apple trees, cabbages coming from cabbage plants? That cannot be accidental; there must be a law. This is not an accidental world. There must be a principle behind it, and that principle is God. If there is a principle, is there ever an exception to the principle? In our system of mathematics two times two is four always, and there is never any exception to that. Does anything grow on apple trees but apples, or on orange trees but oranges?

There is a Principle governing the universe, and because there is a Principle, a divine Law, nothing is ever outside Its government or control, not any more than do the notes of the scale—do, re, mi, fa, sol, la, ti—change in their relationship to one another. No one note has ever crowded another off the scale. No one note has ever infringed upon another. No one note has ever taken anything away from another note.

It is exactly the same with the digits nought, one, two, three, four, five, six, seven, eight, and nine. They never get out of their rightful places; not one of them has ever taken anything from one of the others; not one has ever crowded the other out or drawn from another. Cooperation? Yes, they have cooperated for the common good.

If that is true of mathematics and true of music, how can it be other than true of man who was given dominion over mathematics and music? So, there never has been a man who crowded another man off the earth; there never has been a man who crowded another man out of his business. Never! Those pictures are a part of universal hypnotism, and if we can be made to believe that there is a mortal, material universe, we, too, are a part of this hypnotism. Hypnotism is the error, and we are the ones who have to correct it through the understanding that one with God is a majority. The moment a person knows the truth, or can turn to someone higher in consciousness who can know the truth for him, that "one on God's side is a majority," [2] and that breaks the spell.

[2] Wendell Phillips, *Speech* [*November 1, 1859*].

"GO, AND SIN NO MORE"

The mesmerism may be broken, but that does not mean that the dehypnotized person cannot soon get himself back into it again. If he does not conform to the higher vision, nothing is going to stop him from slipping right back into the same sin, the same disease, or a different one. Jesus said, "Neither do I condemn thee: go, and sin no more." [3] In other words: "I release you and give you your freedom through my understanding of your spiritual nature, but do not go back and indulge in mortality again." If a person who is healed does not change his mode of life, that is, if he goes back and "sins" again, he may find that a worse thing will come upon him.

The world misunderstands the meaning of the word "sin." It means not only getting drunk, committing adultery, or stealing: there is much more to sin than that. *Sin is really the acceptance of a material universe.* Just going back to the belief that there are human beings is the sin that throws a person back into disease and sin again. What the world might call sin—stealing, lying, cheating, and adultery—is of the same nature as disease: it is just another form of hypnotism.

HYPNOTISM IS THE SUBSTANCE OF ALL DISCORD

There is no difference between the hell called poverty and that called war, disease, or sin. One of them is no worse than another. They are all forms of one thing, and that one thing is hypnotism. In one man, hypnotism appears as some sinful thing or thought; in another, it appears as a diseased condition or thought; and in still another, it appears as poverty. The particular form makes no difference; it is all hypnotism. Take away the hypnotism, and none of these things would be there. There is only one error, and that is hypnotism.

[3] John 8:11.

If we can be induced to give treatments to persons—to treat them for nerves or for a mental cause for a physical disease, to treat them for resentment, hatred, jealousy, or anger, or if we can be made to treat them for cancer or consumption—we are not in the practice of spiritual healing: we are in *materia medica* because we are treating effects, whether the effect is a sin, a disease, or poverty, and if we do get rid of it, two more effects lift their heads.

Until we lay the ax at the root of the tree, which is hypnotism, we do not come out of the mortal or material state of consciousness. When we are able to see through the hypnotism, regardless of the name or nature of the sin, disease, or lack, our patient or student will experience harmony, health, wholeness, and completeness. If his trouble is nerves, he finds himself rid of nerves; if his belief is unemployment, he finds himself employed; if his claim is disease, he finds himself well. Why? Because of the practitioner's ability to see through the claim of hypnotism and realize God as the Principle of all that is.

Many times, however, even after a student understands hypnotism to be operating as the suggestion or appearance, he still believes there is a real condition to be destroyed. That is when we hear such expressions as, "Look what hypnotism is doing to me." But hypnotism is not an actual thing or condition. Hypnotism cannot produce water on the desert or snakes in the flowerpot. Hypnotism is itself no thing, no form, no cause, and no effect. Recognizing any form or appearance of error as hypnotism and then dismissing it without any further concern is the correct way to handle all error.

Meditate on this idea of hypnotism as the substance of every form of the mortal or material universe that is appearing to you. When you see sin, disease, lack, and limitation, remember it is hypnotism presenting itself to you as what is called evil form. But then when you see beauty all around, the mountains, ocean, and sunshine, remember that these, too, are forms of hypnotism, only this time appearing to you as good forms.

This does not mean that we are not to enjoy the good of human existence, but rather that we are to enjoy it for what it is—not as something real, in and of itself, but because the reality, that which underlies all good, is spiritual, and must therefore be spiritually discerned. We enjoy the forms of good, knowing them to be temporary forms, not something to be stored up, not something to be put in bank vaults, but something to be enjoyed, and then we go on each day letting the manna fall afresh.

When confronted with the negative aspects of hypnotism, that is, the forms of sin, disease, lack, and limitation, the most important point to remember is that we are not to be fooled by them, not to be fooled into trying to reform evil or sinful persons, but always quickly to remember: "Oh, no! This is hypnotism appearing in still another form, hypnotism which, in and of itself, cannot be the substance, law, cause, or effect of any form of reality." Such a practice enables you to become a spiritual healer.

NEVER TRY TO CHANGE A PERSON OR A CONDITION

As you go further in the work and, through meditation, are able to rise to a point where you are above this world, then you will know me as I am, and I will know you as you are. That is how healings take place, and that is why I caution our students not to tell people that they must correct themselves, not to refuse patients because they do not seem to be doing what they think is right. That has nothing to do with the student. He must go within and see the person he is trying to help as God made him, and then the patient will soon conform "to the pattern shewed to thee in the mount."[4]

The world is hypnotized by person, place, and thing to such

[4] Hebrews 8:5.

a degree that a good person, a good place, and a good thing become so pleasant and comfortable that everybody wants to enjoy these effects, and they do not want to go any higher than that. Such material pleasures and enjoyments cannot be a permanent dispensation, however, because no matter how much good a person may have, he still fluctuates between the pairs of opposites.

So again I say this to you: If you can be made to treat a person in an attempt to change him or give him more of this world's good, or if you can be made to fear war, a depression, or an atomic bomb, you are hypnotized. It is only a question, then, of what date will be placed on your tombstone. If, however, you can catch this vision, when the time comes for you to leave this world, you will step out into a transitional experience which will be higher and better than this one.

You cannot treat a person: you cannot treat a condition. To do that would be like trying to treat the snakes appearing in the flowerpot and saying, "I've got to get rid of my three snakes. As soon as I get rid of them, I'll be able to study better." Do you see how foolish that is? There are not any snakes, so you are never going to get rid of them. All you have to do is to get rid of the hypnotism!

When you really know and believe that—not just believe words—you will no longer have to study truth because the only purpose in studying truth is to learn that hypnotism is the only error, and when you have learned that, there is nothing more to study. All the rest is to be lived within your own being.

The minute you try to change or improve a disease or condition, you yourself are in the hypnotism because there is no disease or condition apart from the mesmerism or the hypnotism. To be ensnared, then, into trying to handle the condition would be but to make the whole situation worse.

Those who are reading or studying truth or who are using truth for healing, for supply, or for some other purpose will find that the more their minds are fixed on getting rid of the condition or on getting the healing, the more are their minds in the mirage of error. You must see that there is no human demonstration to make. There is only one demonstration, and that is gaining the realization of God.

When you have the realization of God, you have all: you have supply; you have immortal life, eternality, and infinity. You cannot demonstrate a home, a companion, a divorce, or a job: you can only demonstrate the presence of God, and that includes whatever the nature of the outward demonstration is to be.

THERE IS NO GOD "AND"

Recognizing the hypnotism includes the demonstration of getting rid of whatever form it might take: the water on the road, the snakes in the flowerpot, or the cancer. But you cannot get rid of these separate and apart from getting rid of the hypnotism. Neither can you make a demonstration of home, employment, or health separate and apart from achieving the conscious realization of God, because there is no demonstration of good separate and apart from God.

There is no use treating person, place, or thing because all there is to error is hypnotism. There is no use seeking a demonstration of person, thing, or condition because there is no demonstration separate and apart from the realization of God. The realization of God includes all demonstrations. "Seek ye first the kingdom of God, and his righteousness; and all these things shall be added unto you." [5]

The important point to understand is that it is the same on the positive side as on the negative. On the positive side, it is demonstrating the consciousness of the presence of God; on the negative side, it is realizing that no matter what the form

5 Matthew 6:33.

of error is, it is hypnotism, and hypnotism alone, which has no substance, law, cause, reality, or effect. These are the two sides of the picture.

The entire basis of The Infinite Way teaching is that there is not God *and*. There is not God *and* health, or God *and* strength, or God *and* immortality, or God *and* activity, or God *and* supply. There is only God manifesting *as*. You can take a block of mahogany, and out of it make a chair, a table, and a bench. But you do not have mahogany *and* a table *and* a chair *and* a bench: you have mahogany manifested or expressed *as* those pieces of furniture.

Therefore, when you think of God as the substance of the universe, you do not have God, the Substance, *and* a variety of forms: you have God appearing or *formed as* these forms, manifested and expressed as form. That is why, if you demonstrate God, you demonstrate every form as which God appears. You demonstrate God as health, as harmony, as immortality, and as supply. You cannot demonstrate God *and* these things, and you cannot demonstrate these things separate and apart from God because they are all God Itself formed.

THERE IS NO HYPNOTISM "AND"

This idea of no separation between the substance of a thing and the thing itself can also be applied to an understanding of all error as hypnotism. There is not hypnotism *and* a disease. There is not hypnotism *and* lack and limitation; there is not hypnotism *and* sin and death. There is only hypnotism *appearing as these pictures*. You cannot get rid of the sin, disease, or death separate and apart from the hypnotism, but when you have rid yourself of hypnotism, you are rid of all its various forms. The way to remove the effects of hypnotism is to understand hypnotism, not as a thing, but as no thing, no power, no presence.

Here you have the secret of living. When, through the senses, you observe life as it seems to be—as you see, hear, taste, touch, or smell it—you understand immediately that this is the product of hypnotism. Through your spiritual sense, however, you discern that right where this human, material, or physical sense seems to be is the spiritual, eternal, and immortal creation.

If you were to see a so-called evil appearance, a sinful, sick, dying, or dead appearance, you would probably be tempted immediately to know some truth that you hope would change the picture, or to think some thought that would heal, correct, improve, or reform it; whereas, if you saw normal human good, normal human wealth, harmony, wholeness, or prosperity, you would most likely accept that picture at its face value.

Hypnotism is just as much hypnotism when it appears as good as when it appears as evil. When you come into a state of life, however, where you can look at the harmonious human appearance and recognize it as hypnotism or appearance or suggestion, and when you can look at the inharmonious or discordant human picture and recognize it as the product of the same hypnotism, as appearance or suggestion, then you have arrived at a point in consciousness in which you will not try to improve, heal, or correct the erroneous picture, nor experience undue satisfaction over the harmonious picture. That is because you will know through your spiritual sense that, regardless of the picture or the nature of its appearance, right there is spiritual reality and harmony, right there eternal and immortal being is. So you will make no mental effort to correct, heal, or improve it. And with that ability to refrain from all attempts to heal, correct, or improve, you will have demonstrated the consciousness of God's allness.

If you can know that the harmonious human appearances are no more real than the inharmonious or discordant ones and if you can know that inharmonious, discordant, sick, sinful, dying human appearances are no more real than harmonious or healthful appearances, then you have arrived at a state of consciousness that spiritually discerns harmony right where any form or human appearance may be.

When you have become accustomed to the idea of observing the harmonious human appearances and the inharmonious human appearances with the same degree of unconcern, you will know that you have arrived at a state of spiritual consciousness in which you see that which is invisible, hear that which is inaudible, and know that which is unknowable. This is Christ-consciousness.

Across the Desk

In March, we traveled to California, and in May we start on another trip through the United States and Europe. Again we will experience the joy of meeting with those who have dedicated themselves to God.

We are ever-mindful of the many revelators of spiritual wisdom whose lives have been consecrated to God's purpose, and of those who have devoted themselves to carrying on their work. Even to think of Zarathustra, Lao-tze, Buddha, Jesus the Christ, and Shankara is to find oneself on holy ground. There are many others, too, who inspire us because we witness the nature of their consecration.

There is another form of dedication which we meet in the lives of those who have surrendered their personal sense of life to give themselves, yes, dedicate themselves, to the cause of freedom, and this is a consecration to loving one's neighbor as himself. These unselfed Souls brought forth the freedom of England, France, Holland, Switzerland, countries in North and South America, as well as others throughout the world.

Many now are devoting themselves to worthy causes in different parts of the world. Some have given themselves to youth in the work of the YMCA and the YWCA, the Boy Scouts and Girl Scouts, to the poor through their work in the Salvation Army, and to the suffering by carrying food and clothing to friendly and enemy countries. Such movements as Care and the Peace Corps demonstrate love in concrete form.

This dedication to God, expressed as consecration to our neighbors' needs ennobles the lives of those who are called and furnishes inspiration to the rest of us so that we, too, may rise above the deadness and dullness of human living. Real living begins only when inspiration enters. Self-completeness is attained only in giving and serving. Freedom is attained in consecration, and peace is found in dedication.

When the Spirit of God touches us, there follows an unrest, a disquiet, a lack of satisfaction with ordinary human experience, and this persists until we find ourselves serving God in our neighbor and resting in Him.

5) Resting in Oneness

It is a grave responsibility when someone comes to you for spiritual help. He is coming to be fed, spiritually fed; he expects help, and you cannot give him a stone. If, at the moment, however, you are not living out from that high consciousness which enables you to give that help, you may reach that state through the process of a contemplative meditation.

This contemplative meditation should consist of every statement that you can bring to conscious remembrance that has to do with the truth that Spirit is the only power—not matter and not mind. Spirit, divine Consciousness, is the only power; invisible Cause is the only power. Dwell upon every truth that will establish in you the conviction that all power is spiritual, all power is invisible, and that there is no power in effect. The truth is that no effect is power, whether that effect appears as a person or a thing.

Many persons wonder how long this meditation should be.

The answer is quite simple. It should continue until you have lost all fear of the condition that has been brought to you for healing. You must continue working with these truths until you feel an inner release, a "click," an inner feeling that tells you that this appearance is only the "arm of flesh," [1] only temporal power, nothingness; and since it is not of God, it has no power. Since it is not of God, it has no life; since it is not of God, it has no continuity, no substance, no being, no externalized form.

When you are able to rest in that realization in complete silence, your meditation is at an end. That does not necessarily mean that your patient is going to be instantaneously healed. True, it is possible for him to be instantaneously healed, but on the other hand his lack of receptivity may not enable him to accept a healing through one realization, two, or even a hundred.

FERTILE SOIL

Many factors enter into the healing that have to do, not so much with you as a practitioner, but with your patients. Sometimes they have been clinging to their conditions for so long that they cannot release them or let them go.

Sometimes, too, a person is not really wholeheartedly wanting God, or the kingdom of God, but has only a desire to get rid of his pain, and no higher object than to become free as soon as possible so as to go out and be a human being again. Such cases are not always broken through easily or quickly. Sometimes there is an absolute rebellion to truth in your patients which you may never discover.

Many different things take place in the consciousness of a person that make it impossible for you to know why he does not respond, even after you have had the inner assurance that

[1] II Chronicles 32:8.

he is healed. If he is patient enough and you are patient enough, eventually a healing will be brought about. Even then, strange as it may seem, it may be a year or two later before a patient comes back to tell you about it, and usually it is because something else has come up, and he wants more help.

The most fertile soil for healing is in the consciousness of a person who has arrived at a place of indifference to the healing, and really feels it is not physical healing about which he is so much concerned as it is experiencing God: living and moving and having his being in the kingdom of God. But how few persons there are who will come to you at that point of readiness!

Your function is not to sit in judgment on the patient, but consciously to realize the presence of God. Each time that you are called upon for help, your meditation should embody whatever truth will bring to you the realization of God as All, and the nothingness of the condition, the nothingness of material or mental law.

Whether it is the second, third, fourth, or one hundredth time you are called upon, you meditate. You do not use a formula, nor do you attempt to recall the last truth you knew. In fact, above all things, you should try to forget that last meditation. Do not believe that the repetition or the recitation of certain truths is going to heal anybody. The purpose of bringing these truths to conscious remembrance is only that you may attain that silence which brings forth the healing.

Every contemplative silence must be spontaneous, and it must be a realization in one way or another of God as Omnipotence, as Omnipresence, as Omniscience. When someone asks for help, you should be able instantly to remember that there is only one power and that this for which he is asking help is not power.

RISE ABOVE BOTH GOOD AND EVIL

Recently, when the principle of one power came up with someone who was drinking too heavily, I cautioned him, "Be careful that you do not believe that alcohol is power, power for good or for evil." At first, that may sound shocking because the devastating effects of alcoholism can be seen on every side, but if you accept the belief that alcohol is power, you will be the blind leading the blind. You will never be able to help anyone rise out of alcoholism unless you, yourself, have clearly perceived the truth that there is only one power. What is the difference, really, between an appearance of alcoholism and an appearance of infectious germs? What is the difference? If you claim that germs have no power, you must be equally sure that alcohol and drugs also have no power.

Your stand from morning to night and night to morning must be that there is but one power. I do not say this lightly. I am well aware of all the appearances there are in the world. I know all the claims to power that exist, but I say to you that, if you are going to live the spiritual life, you must come to the point where Adam and Eve were before they had eaten of the fruit of the tree of the knowledge of good and evil, before they were cast out of the Garden of Eden.

All our discords have to do with our belief that we know what things are good and what things are evil. But there are no *things* that are good, and there are no *things* that are evil. God is the substance of all form, and therefore there is no evil form in all the world. Whether you are ready to accept it or not, the truth is that there also is no good form. There is only God-form, a form that has no opposites. What then are these forms that we behold with the eyes? Concepts, concepts which have been etched into our minds by the belief of good and evil.

"There is nothing either good or bad, but thinking makes it

so." [2] Regardless of what it is that you may call good, the label "good" was given it by some person for some reason, but somewhere on earth there may be those who might call that very same thing bad. Take any form of evil that you know of, and see if you cannot find a place where that very thing is not considered evil. Nothing is good or evil, but thinking makes it so.

Let your contemplative meditation be a rising above both good and evil. Be still, and begin with the premise:

> *There is no power of evil in the world, so I cannot be made to fear this thing. There is God. There must be, and if there is, God could not be God without being infinite, omnipotent, omniscient, and omnipresent. That means that there cannot be anything but God. That means that there cannot be two powers. There is only one.*

Live with the idea until you arrive at a place in consciousness where you know that there are not two powers, and when you reach that place, you are back in the Garden of Eden, and you have taken your patient there with you.

DWELLING IN OMNIPOTENCE, OMNIPRESENCE, AND OMNISCIENCE

Repeating words will be of little effect: you must take the words into your consciousness and let the depth of their meaning be revealed:

> *All power! What power am I dealing with if God is all power? Is there any power in this so-called patient, even a power to resist this treatment? If God is the only power operating as the consciousness of this person, is there any other*

[2] William Shakespeare. *Hamlet*, Act II, Sc. 2.

power? Is there any power in what the world calls a disease or an enemy?

And so you meditate on what really constitutes power until material or mental power has lost all significance to you, and you are left with the realization and the assurance, *"I in the midst of you am mighty. I am the only power."*

In the next meditation you have for the very same person or the very same condition, you may take the word "omnipresence."

> *God is omnipresence. But what does that mean? If God is omnipresence, it must mean that God is the presence of this patient. There can be no presence of a patient other than the presence of God. There can be no presence of a disease, since God alone is omnipresence, and God is Spirit. God is the presence of this person; God is the presence of all there is because God is the only presence.*

> *God does not have to be removed, healed, corrected, reformed, or improved. Because God is omnipresence, I know that there is no such presence as a patient, a sin, a disease, a false appetite, or even a material or mental law.*

That realization, however, may not bring about the healing either. And so you come to the word "omniscience," which means all-knowledge, all-science, all-wisdom.

> *God is omniscience. I do not have to tell the all-knowing God anything about my patient or his condition. If God does not know it now, God never will, and surely I could not be guilty of such egotism as to believe that I know something God does not know. Therefore, I do not have to tell God anything about my patient, what my patient needs or requires, or what my patient would like. I only have to sit here and know that God is omniscience, the all-knowing intelligence.*

The Father knows what things I have need of, and it is His "good pleasure to give [me] the kingdom." [3] *How wonderful it is to be able to sit here and not have to tell God something about my patient! How wonderful to know that all that is to be known God already knows, and God already knows what to do and when to do it and how to do it.*

In your contemplative meditation, you continue to remember every passage of Scripture and every passage of spiritual literature that brings to you the assurance and the reassurance that God already knows the need, and then rest in that until you have an inner feeling that all is well.

A healing meditation is complete only if it embodies the truth about God: God's law, God's omnipotence, God's omniscience, God's omnipresence. Then, even though the patient may have a high fever, may be in pain, distress, or poverty, everything of a fearful nature is eradicated from your thought, and an inner feeling of assurance comes to you:

This is God's beloved child. What then have I to fear? Is there a child of God outside the kingdom of God, or am I being fooled by appearances? That must be where the difficulty lies. I have been fooled into believing in appearances because my eyes and my ears testify to a selfhood outside the kingdom of God.

THERE IS NOT GOD "AND" A PATIENT

Are you going to judge by what you see, hear, taste, touch, and smell? Are you going to believe that God is in that picture? If you are going to look at this world with your eyes, you are never going to be able to believe in God because all you can see, hear, taste, touch, and smell is finiteness, just finiteness: limitation, sin, disease, death, stupidity. Once you close your eyes to

[3] Luke 12:32.

the appearance and ask yourself, "What is the kingdom of God like? What is the Garden of Eden?" you will hear the still small voice, and even while you are looking directly at sick, sinning, or dying man, that voice will say to you:

> *"This is my beloved Son, in whom I am well pleased."* [4]
> Fear not, it is I.

> I, God, constitute all being in spite of every appearance to the contrary. There is only one I. Therefore, *"It is I; be not afraid."* [5]

But do not look with your eyes because you will be deceived. *I* is in you, and *I* is in me. We are one. There is room in heaven only for *I*. There is room only for One, and that One is God. You would be surprised at what sometimes happens in meditation when you realize that there is no room in the kingdom of God for God *and* your patient; and since there is nothing but the kingdom of God, your fear drops away. You realize:

> *I have been looking with my eyes; I have been believing what my eyes see, believing sense testimony. I have been judging by appearances, when in reality there is only God. There is but the* I *which I am.*

KEEP YOUR MEDITATION AND PRAYER CENTERED
ON GOD

Always begin your meditation with a contemplation of truth, but by this time you know that there is no truth about "man, whose breath is in his nostrils." [6] So there is no use pondering or contemplating anything about your patient or his condition. If, then, you are not to take your patient or his condition into

4 Matthew 3:17.
5 John 6:20.
6 Isaiah 2:22.

your meditation, what are you to do? There is nothing left but God. Therefore, in your contemplative meditation, you meditate on God:

God! Why am I seeking God, when God is already closer to me than breathing? Why am I struggling so hard to reach God? Why am I going through so many mental gymnastics? Why do I think I have to repeat formulas? Why should I believe that I have to stand on my head, or fast, or feast to find the God that is already my very own being? True, judging from appearances, I am separate and apart from God, but what is the truth? What truth is there other than that I and the Father are one?

God is; I am. I am not meditating to find God. I am meditating only to bring to conscious remembrance the truth that I and the Father are one, that the place whereon I stand is holy ground. All that God is, I am, for He has said, "Son, thou art ever with me, and all that I have is thine." [7]

Here and now all that the Father has is mine: wisdom, life, love, peace, confidence, serenity, and joy. I need not struggle physically or mentally for these. I need not go any place to find them because here where I am God is—I in God, and God in me.

This is the truth about me; this is the truth about my patient; this is the truth about my family. There is really no family but God's family since there is only one Father: "Call no man your father upon the earth: for one is your Father, which is in heaven." [8] *We are all of one household.*

God in the midst of me is my life, the bread on my table, the meat and the wine and the water. God "is the health of my countenance." [9]

[7] Luke 15:31.
[8] Matthew 23:9.
[9] Psalm 42:11.

I do not have to go anywhere; I do not have to think anything. "Be still, and know that I am God." [10] *I is God. I is infinite. I is all-inclusive. In the presence of the I, there is fulfillment.*

Where the Spirit of the I is, there is peace, joy, completeness, and harmony. I do not have to deserve it: God's rain falls alike on the just and on the unjust. I have only to be still because it is "not by might, nor by power" [11] *that this is realized: it is "in quietness and in confidence."* [12] *In quietness and confidence, I know the presence of God is here with me even though I cannot feel It.*

THE RETURN TO THE FATHER'S HOUSE IS AN ACTIVITY OF CONSCIOUSNESS

Does God have a son and then disinherit him? Does God have a son and cast him off? No, even the Prodigal was able to find his way back to the realization of God—not by traveling anywhere in time or space, but by making a journey in consciousness. So, too, you do not have to go any place in time or space. The spiritual journey that you are making is being made in consciousness. It all takes place in your consciousness where you come to the conscious remembrance:

I and the Father are one. Even if I make my bed in hell, even if "I walk through the valley of the shadow of death," [13] *I and the Father are one. Neither life nor death can separate me from the life of God, the love of God, the awareness of God, the presence and the power of God. "I will never leave thee, nor forsake thee."* [14] *Never leave thee, never! I will be "with you alway, even unto the end of the world."* [15]

[10] Psalm 46:10.
[11] Zechariah 4:6.
[12] Isaiah 30:15.
[13] Psalm 23:4.
[14] Hebrews 13:5.
[15] Matthew 28:20.

You must bring back to your consciousness a remembrance of all the spiritual truth that you have ever read in Scripture or in mystical and spiritual writings. Everything must take place as an activity of consciousness because the journey from the Prodigal's feast with the swine back to the Father's house and to the awareness of Omnipotence, Omnipresence, and Omniscience is a journey made in consciousness.

No one can attain this awareness for you. You must attain it through a conscious realization of all the spiritual truth you have ever known, and you must continue in your meditation or prayer—call it what you will—until such time as fear departs from you. Then you can sit "in quietness and in confidence" and let God's grace flow through you. Let the voice of God speak to you if it will; let the voice of God thunder if it will, or just breathe into your ear a "peace be still," a "be not afraid; it is I." What have you to fear, if I is with you? And that I never will leave you, nor forsake you—not in purity and not in sin, not in health and not in disease, not in life and not in death. I was with you before you were born, and I will be with you to the end of the world.

If I is closer to you than breathing, you are in God's presence, and can you ask any more than that? Can you desire anything other than to be in God's presence? So fear drops away, and from somewhere deep down within you comes a release. And when that happens, you have no more fear because you are in the presence of God. You have attained that mind that was in Christ Jesus, that mind in which there is no fear.

NEVER TAKE A PERSON INTO MEDITATION

The purpose of meditation is to bring you into conscious union with God, but when it is for the purpose of *helping* yourself or others, it can be called contemplative meditation, which sometimes carries with it the sense of overcoming even if it is not intended to do so. When you contemplate God or when your meditation consists of knowing all the truth about God and spiritual creation, then you are really in the mystical way of life and the spiritual way of healing.

In a healing meditation, you never project your thought to your patient, never under any circumstance, because, if you did, you would be trying to patch up the illusion. To do this is nothing more nor less than mental power projected, which is a form of suggestive therapy. It is healing by suggestion, and suggestion is a mild form of hypnotism, neither of which has anything to do with spiritual healing. You never address your patient by name, nor do you ever say "you" to your patient. Your meditation has nothing to do with your patient: it has to do only with you and your relationship with God and your awareness of God. Because your patient has reached out to you for help, he will get the benefit of your realized oneness with God.

It is not statements of truth that bring about healing. If they did, you would never outgrow statements of truth, and the day will come when you will outgrow them. Statements of truth are for the purpose of reinforcing your own understanding and assurance, so that you can come to a place of "relaxedness," and then wait for the Spirit to announce Itself. You cannot do that while you are fearing for your patient. You cannot do that while you are wondering what can help him or how you can reach God. You can rest in an inner peace only after you have come to the realization that there are not powers of good and powers of evil: there is only the power of God. You cannot rest in your meditation until you have reached a consciousness in which there are not two powers, two laws, or two substances operating.

STAND FAST IN THE PRINCIPLE OF ONENESS

At times, you may be presented with a problem of some kind of a law: a law of heredity, a law of infection or contagion, a law of time or age, or some legal law. And so you sit in your meditation:

Law, law! God is the only lawgiver, and God is Spirit. Then all law must be spiritual. How can there be a destructive law? How can there be a finite law? How can there be a law of limitation?

There is only one law, and it is spiritual. There are no material laws; there are no laws that are binding on the son of God.

Even legal laws cannot bind anyone in the presence of spiritual Grace. The only law is the law of Spirit, and the very moment that Spirit touches even a person in prison, the penalty of violating the legal law drops away, and the prisoner is free. A spiritual being cannot be held in any kind of prison, and when a person has been touched by the Spirit he has "died" to his humanhood and has been reborn of the Spirit. How can such a one be held in prison?

On another occasion, you may be told that your patient is going to die and that nothing can be done to save him. With that, the word "power" may come into your mind, "Power to cause death? Power to perpetuate disease? Power? Power? Power?" until that word rings in you, and you realize, "God is power. If God is power, can there be two powers? What, then, have I to fear? I shall not fear what power can do to me."

THE ONLY PROBLEM IS THE BELIEF THAT THE CARNAL MIND IS A POWER

Always remember this: your patient is not suffering from rheumatism; he is not suffering from a cold; he is not suffering from a headache: he is suffering from the universal acceptance of the carnal mind as a power. Consciously or unconsciously, he has accepted two powers, the power of God *and* the power of error called carnal mind. To nullify error in your experience, in your family's, patient's, or student's experience, you see through the belief that the carnal mind is power.

You have only one demonstration to make, and that is the realization of the presence of God. You have only one devil to overcome, and it is not rheumatism, cancer, consumption, immorality, poverty, or unemployment. Do not pray for employment for an unemployed person. Remember, it is the carnal mind claiming that there is lack and limitation, lack of opportunity or lack of some other thing. Then realize that carnal mind is not power and that there is no lack in God's kingdom. If business is not good, do not pray for good business. Pray to realize that the carnal mind and its suggestions are not power.

We have a principle that works, and the principle is this: There is only one demonstration to make: the consciousness of the presence of God, for in Its presence the carnal mind dissolves. There is only one sin, disease, death, lack, or limitation: the carnal mind. Whether you call it carnal mind or some other name makes no difference. In my writings, you will find carnal mind referred to under the name of hypnotism, suggestion, mesmerism, world belief, or appearance. They all mean the same thing: a belief that there is a destructive power.

That is all we are suffering from: a belief in two powers which, consciously or unconsciously, all of us have accepted. Suppose you became convinced this instant that God is the only power. Then what could trouble you? Nothing! A whole circus full of wild lions could be turned loose in this room, and you would not get up to move out of the way. What difference would it make even if they were there if there is only one power? If bombs were falling right and left, what difference would it make to you if there is only one power? *If* there is only one power, what can bombs do? Or wild lions, or germs, or weather, or climate?

Your meditation does not become effective until you, yourself, arrive at the place of oneness: one power, one law, one presence, one life, one being, one cause, and one effect. Then you can wait for God's grace to be upon you, God's Spirit to envelop you, and God's release to come to you. When that comes, your meditation is complete.

Never forget that your meditation is not complete until you arrive at the place of inner peace through the realization of One—whether it is one power, one person, one cause, or one law—always One. When you come to that place in your own consciousness, you are at peace, and very soon the grace of God will be upon you.

This peace does not always come with your first meditation. You may have to meditate again for your patient an hour or two or three hours later, or you may have to repeat it that night, or in the middle of the night, or the next morning. You may have to repeat it for days and days. This is because, as human beings, we are living a life of separation from God, and it is not always easy at any or every moment we choose to get at-one with God. So it is that it may be necessary to meditate many times until the "click" finally comes that sets us free.

The simplicity of the message of The Infinite Way lies in the truth that you have only one enemy. And it is not carnal mind! It is the *belief* that carnal mind is power, and when you have overcome the belief that it is power, it is finished as far as you are concerned. Then you do not have to demonstrate supply; you do not have to demonstrate health; you do not have to demonstrate happiness; you do not have to demonstrate companionship: you demonstrate only the realized presence of God. All that you need is God's grace realized, and It fulfills Itself in all things.

Across the Desk

Spring is here as I write this, and therefore my thought turns to renewal, rebirth, and resurrection, and how these may be experienced. There is one necessary step without which we cannot "die" out of the old and be reborn into the new man, the risen man.

Write this on your forehead where you will see it every time you go to the mirror: God does not care how much of a sinner you are or how pure you may be. God has no interest in your humanhood: saint or sinner, well or sick, rich or poor.

It is up to you to turn away from your present state of consciousness which may be expressing as sainthood or sinfulness, and focus your attention on the recognition of the spiritual nature of individual being. When you can forget my humanhood and behold the Christ of me, the Christ of you will rise. When you forgive—release others from the penalty of their sins—your penalty will dissolve.

Do not wait to become good before seeking God because you will not find Him. It is not easy to acknowledge your own Christhood because you know your human failings so well. Therefore, recognize the Christ of those you meet, and then come face to face with the risen Christ of your Self.

Cease seeing me or any person as a man of earth, and meet yourself as the Christ-man. Release everyone from his past, and come face to face with your *now*—your moment of Christhood. This does not mean that when you hire an employee you will not seek the best qualified person, or that when you go to the polls you will not vote for the candidate who most nearly fits your idea of rightness. You will use discrimination, but you will also release man from condemnation, and thereby discover your own freedom. Be assured, you attain freedom *only* as you free others; you attain justice only as you are just; you attain abundance only as you give.

You admit the Christ, the Spirit of God, into your consciousness as you recognize the Christ in man. "I stand at the door, and knock." [16] When you admit *Me,* the Christ, *I* am then come that you might have abundant life. That *I* then becomes the bread and meat of life to you, the wine of inspiration and the pure waters of life eternal. Open the door of your consciousness and admit the Spirit of God, and then the Christ lives your life.

Have you ever felt that there is a *Me,* a real tangible *Me,* closer to you than breathing? If not, begin to greet *Me* in all whom you meet, especially the enemy, and quickly you will meet *Me* in you.

[16] Revelation 3:20.

6) *Living the Principle of Impersonalization*

To different people, and for many different reasons, travel is a stimulating and fascinating activity, but in my experience the main function of travel has been to meet people. My interest has always been in people. I have seen all the scenery, sometimes once and sometimes many times and I have seen the art galleries, too. But I like people, and I do not go around the world over and over again to see more scenery or even to see more art galleries, but to meet people. Life is for living, and the living cannot be done except it is done with others. No one can live a life unto himself and be fulfilled, and no nation, race, or creed can live unto itself and become anything but ingrown.

The more traveling there is, the more opportunity there is for a meeting of minds and for a greater understanding of others, even on the human level. Think what it would mean to the world if, in our contact with other people, we could attain the awareness that everyone is the temple of the living God, if we were no longer to ascribe evil to one another, no longer believe that evil is a component part of this or that race, of this or that nation, but were to learn to impersonalize. Think of the kind of relationships that could exist in the world if we were to embody these spiritual principles. Think of the invisible bond that would be established among all peoples of the world through such spiritual illumination.

These principles will never become effective on a world-wide scale, however, unless you and I begin applying them where we are in our home, here and now. Let us assume that there is a member of your family who is not living up to the highest standards of humanhood, much less of his spiritual identity, a person who is unruly, disobedient, dishonest, untruthful, untrustworthy, unfaithful, or one who is not measuring up to the standard of normal health, physically or mentally.

Surely, it must be clear to you that you have a responsibility in your own home. True, you are not necessarily responsible for the purity of everyone in your home, nor is it your responsibility that everyone there conform to your standards of life, since one of the privileges of living in a free country is that each person is an individual and has the right to live his own life.

This is true, however, only up to a certain point. Each and every person is entitled to liberty, but not to license. There are things that no one should tolerate in his home. Remember that your home is your domain, and you should permit nothing to enter that home "that defileth . . . or maketh a lie." [1] Therefore, it is your function to prevent the entrance of whatever may disturb your household, or to eliminate it after it is there, in other words, to bring about a change in the situation.

[1] Revelation 21:27.

CHANGING THE ATMOSPHERE OF YOUR HOME

To each one of us, then, comes this question: "How can I change the atmosphere of my home? How can I improve it? And, even if it is humanly good, how can I lift it above human goodness into the demonstration of spiritual harmony, spiritual health, spiritual purity, spiritual abundance?"

It is at this point that you bring the three basic principles of The Infinite Way into operation. First of all, you must realize that it makes no difference whether at the moment you are looking at a person in sin, disease, or nearing death. The truth is that God constitutes individual being. God is the quality, God is the quantity, God is the essence, and God is the law unto every person in your household. God constitutes his being; and therefore, his nature is pure, godly, good.

With that thoroughly established in your consciousness, you can turn to the second step, which is the most important principle of all, impersonalization. Whether a member of your family is suffering from sickness, sin, false appetite, unemployment, lack, bad disposition, hate, envy, jealousy, or malice, the all-important step is to impersonalize the error. *You must impersonalize.* You must be able to look at that individual, realizing that the only nature there is, is godly. This sin, this disease, this whatever it may be is not of a person. It has its source in the carnal mind. This of which he is a victim, this which is manifesting itself in him, on him, through him, or as him, this actually is an activity or substance of the carnal mind or devil.

Does that not contradict much of what you have been thinking about this person? Perhaps, because of your previous metaphysical background, you have been probing into his consciousness, seeking to find the error so that you could remove it. You may have been blaming his religious beliefs, or his lack of them, or in some way or other you may have been attempting to eradicate the error from him. By now you must understand that it is impossible to do that because the error is not, and never was, a part of his being. God constitutes his being, and God has constituted his being from everlasting to everlasting.

Let me remind you again that it is for this reason that you must never use the name of a person in treatment, nor must you ever name the disease or the problem because you are then personalizing it and fastening it to the very individual you would like to see free. It is vitally important for you to understand that this trait or quality of character, this apparently evil nature, this false appetite, or this diseased condition is an activity of the carnal mind.

Therefore, when you have impersonalized whatever the problem may be to the extent that you really have released the individual and can feel that this is something that does not belong to him, but something that exists only in the carnal mind, you then take the third and final step and realize:

> There is only one mind, the mind that is the instrument of God. Therefore, there is no carnal mind or mortal mind. That which has been termed carnal mind is not a mind at all: it is a belief in two powers. When there is no belief in two powers, there is no carnal mind.

In other words, if you could wholly remove from yourself the belief in two powers, as far as you are concerned, there would be no human beings left to be healed or improved. There would be only children of God, or Adam and Eve in the Garden of Eden before they ate of the fruit. All there is to humanhood is a belief in two powers. Without that belief, there is no human race any more: there is only immortal being.

LOVING YOUR NEIGHBOR BY LIVING THE PRINCIPLES

After you have practiced these three principles in your home and have begun to see some changes, you broaden your horizon by practicing them when you go to market, to your business office or factory, or when you are driving an automobile or riding in a bus.

The moment you leave your home, you are faced with countless pictures of carnal mind: drunkenness, obscenity, vice, mean disposition, poverty, deformity. You cannot pass by on the other side of the road. You have to be the one who ministers to those persons so afflicted—only in order to do this you do not have to leave whatever it is you are doing. All you have to do is to recognize:

> *God constitutes all being; therefore, the nature of man is godly. Even the body is the temple of the living God. Body, mind, Soul, and Spirit—these are the temple of the living God, and this that I am seeing or hearing is carnal mind, the "arm of flesh,"* [2] *nothingness. It is a belief in two powers.*
>
> *Thank You, Father, that I know enough to know that there is only one power, one mind, one life, one law; and that power, mind, life, and law are spiritual.*

In this meditation or treatment, you have not treated any person; you have not used anyone's name or identified his fault; you have not directed a treatment to him. All this was a truth realized within you *about the appearance*. It does not matter who the appearance is or what the appearance is: it is nothing but an appearance, and you are recognizing it as the carnal mind, the "arm of flesh," or nothingness—and you can rest in that word.

[2] II Chronicles 32:8.

SECRECY

It will not take long for you to discover that you are having experiences different from any you have ever had before, and that a change is taking place within you. But here I must caution you about something both in your home and outside of it. Be sure that all this is taking place in secret. Never voice this to anyone. No one must ever be told; no one must ever know that you are knowing the truth.

The day does come, however, when someone in your family says, "You have changed," or "You know something," and then, if you find that he is really serious in wanting to know what has brought about the change in you, you can begin to impart what you have learned. But you have to be very, very sure that he really wants to know, that he is not going to let you unburden yourself and then ridicule it, and thereby probably deprive you of your "pearl." Be very sure that you treat this truth as the "pearl of great price." [3] If anyone comes to you for it, be sure that he is coming to you in humility and in earnestness, that he is coming to you really and truly seeking, and not just out of curiosity.

Until a person is well grounded in these principles, it does not take much for him to lose what little awareness he has gained and the benefit of it. When people mock, scorn, or deride his study or beliefs, it begins to undermine his faith, and unless he has beheld its activity and witnessed its fruits time and time again he can be made to waver. Many persons have. Like Lot's wife, they sometimes look back if they do not know the principles thoroughly, and if they have not seen them work so often that nothing, not even crucifixion, could make them change their minds.

[3] Matthew 13:46.

EVIL IS IMPERSONAL

Always remember that, whatever belief you or I may be suffering from, it is not your belief or mine: it is a universal belief which we have temporarily picked up, accepted, or to which we have yielded. Never blame anyone and never try to make anyone better than he is. You will not succeed, and you will only give yourself heartaches. It is useless to tell a person to be more loving, more generous, or more forgiving because he cannot be anything more than he is, until a change of consciousness takes place through the realization that any undesirable qualities he seems to possess never were of him. They are of the carnal mind: they are not, and never were, power; and they operate only because of the universal belief in two powers.

If you see a man stealing, do not call him a thief. Realize instantly, "This is a belief in two powers operating, but it cannot operate because there are not two powers." If you do this, you will not only heal youself, but you will be loving your neighbor as yourself—and that is important. If for any reason you might be tempted to steal, and someone should see you, surely the one thing you would most appreciate would be for that person to know that you are not a thief, that you were but responding to an impersonal impulse, and that it is not power. If such truth were known for you when assailed by temptation, probably you would stop right in the midst of the act.

When we live in this higher consciousness, we are living in an entirely different atmosphere, in a world where we are not conscious of the evil traits in people, or even the erroneous ones. We are far more aware of the good qualities that are being expressed. This is in no wise a Pollyanna attitude because when we are in the consciousness of God as the only Being, then the evil that may be presented to us as a person dissolves, and we bring to that person a higher and richer experience than he knew before—especially if he is at all receptive to the spiritual way of life.

This has been proved to a large degree in the work that I have carried on in prisons. It was while I was working with the inmates in a prison that I first became aware of the principle that there is no evil, as such, in people, not even in those who are in prison.

Several years ago, I was invited to speak to a group of prisoners who had found a couple of Infinite Way pamphlets through one of the teachers working in the prison. Evidently these pamphlets had been circulated rather widely because I found a good-sized group of men waiting to hear me. Before I went into the room where the men were assembled, the man in charge of such activities called me aside and said, "You're in trouble, and I'm going to get you out of it. There are sixty-six men in there waiting for you, but I've read *The Infinite Way,* so I can tell you that they don't want anything you've got. I have an idea you will be able to hold them for about ten minutes, so when you find yourself slipping, just look at me and give me a wink, and I will call for a smoking recess, and then I'll have someone else take over."

"All right," I replied. "I'll be on the alert."

One hour passed, and there was not a sound in that room. By then, the man in charge was beginning to wonder what it was all about and called a recess for smoking, but the men said, "Can't we smoke and have you go on with your talk?" Two hours passed, and then he announced that the time was up. He told me afterward that he was astounded that these prisoners had displayed such a deep interest in, and could be so attentive to, a talk of this nature.

Actually, the secret was what I had learned in my first experience in prison work, and that was that there are no sinful men. There is no such thing as evil in the mind of man. Evil is absolutely impersonal. Man, himself, is an incarnation of God.

God is the very fiber and fabric of man's being, and everything else is superimposed upon that perfect expression. It is not any more a part of man's spiritual identity than dirt is a part of the water in a pail. Even after the dirt gets into the water, it can always be removed because it never becomes water.

Evil never becomes man, nor does it become a part of man. Whatever appears to be there can be removed by anyone who realizes the impersonal nature of the appearance. That has been the secret of The Infinite Way in working with every form of sin, false appetite, disease, and all the other inharmonies that come into human experience.

There is not one of us who has a fault—and we all have them—who would not be grateful if the members of our family who know our faults, instead of blaming us or trying to reform us, would silently, secretly, and sacredly know this truth, "This is an impersonal belief in two powers, just an impersonal claim of a power apart from God. There is no mind but that mind which is the instrument of God; therefore, carnal mind is not enmity against God. It is nothing. Carnal mind is a belief in two powers, a universal belief. It is not my belief. It has no person in whom, on whom, or through whom to operate."

Practice, practice, practice, until you can look at the saint or the sinner and know that the saint never could be a saint any more than the sinner could be a sinner. Do not make the mistake of saying that there is no evil, but that all is good. Good and evil are just two ends of the same stick. "Why callest thou me good?" [4] Do not call anyone good. Do not forget that there are no saints. God alone is good.

When a person is showing forth any measure of goodness, be assured that it is only God expressing through him. The part for which a person deserves credit is that he is willing to be a transparency, and thereby he plays his role in this work. No individual can be good: God alone is good, but that goodness

[4] Matthew 19:17.

must find expression as individual being. Once you perceive that, you will find it very easy never to judge, criticize, or condemn an individual because you will know that whatever evil is present is nothing more nor less than a universal belief in good and evil. If that individual does not know enough to annihilate that belief, you can help to do it for him, more especially if he is reaching out for help.

THE SIGNIFICANCE OF ANANIAS AND SAPPHIRA

Any person who lives and moves and has his being in the realization of God's presence as Omnipotence is living in one power, and there is no secondary power that can touch him. Whether that power is in the form of a mental projection, a germ, a hereditary condition, infection or contagion, age, or what not, rest assured that no individual who is living in the life of Oneness—one power, one law, one being, one cause— can be the victim of malpractice.

Many persons misunderstand the meaning of the term "malpractice." They believe that if someone hates, dislikes, or mistrusts them or if a person is directing evil thoughts toward them, his hatred, dislike, mistrust, or evil thought acts as a form of malpractice, and may have a harmful effect upon them. Undoubtedly, this does operate wherever there is a belief in two powers, but be assured that the only power it has is the power they give it. To the person who knows that there is no one to malpractice or be malpracticed, and who thereby impersonalizes it, any evil that comes knocking at his door will not touch him: it will only backfire to the one who sent it.

That is really the significance of the story of Ananias and Sapphira. After the Crucifixion, the disciples were so persecuted that they were forced to go underground. They were unable to earn a livelihood, so they banded together and agreed to put into one fund all that they owned, thereby helping to support one another out of this common fund until the period of persecution passed. This they all did and gave the fund over to the care of Peter for safekeeping. Sapphira and her husband, however, decided to hold out a little of what they had, a deception which Peter was quick to discern. When he rebuked them, "Thou hast not lied unto men, but unto God," [5] what he really was saying was that there is no man, but only God-Selfhood, and that their act of deception was unto God, the consequences of which were so great that both Sapphira and her husband dropped dead.

The very moment they consciously wronged God, the evil whanged back on them and destroyed them. God did not cause this; God did not do this: the evil that they committed against that little band of disciples hit up against the Selfhood of God which is invisible and incorporeal. There was nothing there and nobody to receive it, so it had to boomerang right back to the senders. Thus it is that the evil that is directed against man is really being directed against God. But when there is nothing in man but the Christ-Spirit, there is nothing for evil to strike at, and it boomerangs and destroys the sender.

In thinking of the episode of Sapphira and her husband, it is important to remember that it was not really Sapphira and her husband who held out their savings from God. It was the carnal mind. So, too, with us: it is not we who are evil. It is the carnal mind operating through us, and inasmuch as this carnal mind is not a person and has no person in whom, through whom, or upon whom to operate, it becomes a nothingness. When we impersonalize it and begin to understand that no person has done any evil unto us because there is no "us" separate from God—we have no Selfhood but the capital "S" Selfhood —and therefore no one has wronged or injured us, no one has

[5] Acts 5:4.

aimed any evil at us, but at God, we will find that we have so impersonalized our own self and all others that any human error that is directed toward us will not strike us.

Then if we remember, also, that those who aim evil in our direction are not really aiming it at all, but that they are merely instruments through which the carnal mind is operating, we shall more than likely release them from their sin and bring about their forgiveness. In other words, if we impersonalize evil and recognize that it has not been done unto us, it may turn around and strike back at the sender. If it did, it would probably be his fault in the sense of permitting himself to be used.

We want to go higher, however, than being avenged or wreaking vengeance upon someone: we want to see those who do evil to us forgiven and released from whatever evil is holding them in its grasp.

If there is any ingratitude directed toward us, or any lack of mercy or justice, we realize first of all our capital "S" Self and then realize that, because of that, this is not aimed at us at all: it is aimed at God. Furthermore, by realizing that it is never a person who is aiming evil in our direction, but that he is merely the innocent victim of the carnal mind, a victim of ignorance, we can truthfully repeat, "Father, forgive him, for he knows not what he does," and then we can realize that this carnal mind is a nothingness. Thus we nullify it, and we shall then discover how quickly we come into our freedom. There is a joyous freedom when we are living in a world where no one has anything against us, and if there does seem to be anyone, we have now recognized that it is not person, but an impersonal source which is really not power.

This act of impersonalization is a conscious one. Eventually, it will make clear to us why we could sit around from now until doomsday praying to God for something, and it will not come. We could pray for justice or cooperation or gratitude from now to the end of time and not get it. In other words, good can come into our experience only through an act of our own consciousness. There is no God outside our being to see that we get mercy, justice, or kindness.

THE UNIVERSALITY OF THE DIVINE SELFHOOD

In our meditations, let us impersonalize the evils of this world and begin to know that we are not the source of evil to anyone because God constitutes the selfhood of our being. Moreover, no person is the avenue or channel of evil toward us, for God constitutes his selfhood, and any evil apparent in our world is a product of the universal carnal mind which, in and of itself, is nothing until we accept a person as an outlet for its activity. The responsibility is ours. The Master said, "Ye shall know the truth, and the truth shall make you free," [6] but he did not say that the truth would make us free without our *knowing* the truth.

As we sow, so shall we reap. All harmony and success in life are up to the individual, and to sow to the Spirit means to impersonalize to the extent that we realize God as the true identity, not only of every human being, but of every animal and every plant.

God is the life of all of us, and that Life does not begin or end with a human being. The life of God is infinite; the life of God is the life of you and of me, of animals, vegetables, and minerals. Even the rocks and the stones are living things; they are not inanimate as they appear to be, but they live and breathe, and God is the life and breath of their being.

This, too, is impersonalizing. It is making God the divine Self, the Self of you and the Self of me and the Self of all living things in the universe. For most of us, it will be necessary to meditate on this day in and day out until its truth begins to

[6] John 8:32.

unfold from within ourselves, until we gain the conviction of it and something wells up within us and says, "This really is true. This is the truth of being. God does constitute my Selfhood, and therefore my Selfhood is not subject to hate, envy, jealousy, or wrong thinking. My Selfhood is intact in God. My Selfhood is divine, immortal being."

As you meditate upon this, it will not be too long before you will begin to see fruitage appear. Remember, the promise is that you are to bear fruit richly because of your identification with God, your Father within you.

Once this has been established in you, you now have to begin secretly, silently, and very sacredly to look around at the members of your household and at your friends and begin to change your concepts of them so that you realize that all this that you have been declaring of yourself is likewise true of them. They, too, are one with this divine Selfhood. The fact that at the moment they do not know it is not your concern. You are not dealing with their demonstration but with your own, and you will not have any kind of demonstration unless you begin to perceive that this truth that you have declared and realized about yourself must be a universal truth.

ALL MALPRACTICE IS SELF-MALPRACTICE

Regardless of any person's lack of demonstration, regardless of his unwillingness even to want to learn about his true identity, you are secretly and silently knowing the truth. You are knowing the true identity of your employers, employees, your customers or clients, and the officials of the government. It makes no difference what these persons may seem to be or may seem to be doing. You are now realizing their oneness with their Source. This is not for the purpose of giving them a treatment, but just to save yourself from being a malpractitioner because unless you are seeing people as they really are, you are malpracticing them, and your malpractice eventually comes home to roost. Your malpractice of other persons never harms them, and their malpractice of you never harms you.

Any malpractice acts as a boomerang: it goes out from us and eventually hits nothing because it is aimed only at our *concept* of a person—not at the person—and therefore it turns around and returns and cuts our heads off. It never strikes those at whom it is aimed. It always turns around and reacts upon the sender.

Not all malpractice is malicious; not all malpractice is intended to harm someone; but unless you are seeing everybody, even your enemies—and this is the meaning of praying for your enemies—as one with God, unless you are seeing that Self with a capital "S" as the true identity of everyone, you are malpracticing. Unless you can do this, you are setting up a special hierarchy consisting of your friends and you, all of whom are perfect in your eyes, and all the rest of the people in the world are not. This is not true.

The truth is that we are all one in Christ Jesus; we are all the offspring of God. None of us has a human father. There is but one Father in this universe, and that is God. All of us are offspring of that one creative Principle, and we are malpracticing when we do not live this truth. To recognize the truth of oneness is to impersonalize our sense of self as applied to yourself and myself and as applied to all the people of this world, including our enemies.

What happens when you have sufficiently meditated on this truth so that you do not recognize any selfhood apart from God? Could you possibly suffer loss or destruction from another? Could you ever be the victim of injustice, inequality, or any evil if there is no selfhood other than God?

This principle of oneness can be applied in cases at law where individuals are seeking justice. Unless the person involved in litigation is seeing God as his Selfhood and as the

Selfhood of judge, jury, and attorneys, how can he possibly expect justice? Can justice, equity, or mercy come from "man, whose breath is in his nostrils"? [7] Anyone who looks for it in that quarter is likely to be very much disappointed. In all our relationships in life, unless we are looking to the divine Self of all being for our good, we are looking amiss and we may not find it.

Meditation on this subject will eventually bring a person the conscious awareness that God constitutes the Selfhood of every individual. So, whether he is seeking justice in court, from his employer, or from a labor union, he must be sure that he is expecting that justice from the divine Selfhood of individual being and that he is recognizing God as that Selfhood. When he does that, he will have impersonalized the good he hopes for and the evil he fears.

Whenever we have a grievance against anyone, we are faced with the belief of injustice from that person or a lack of mercy or cooperation; and in accepting that, we are pinning the evil on him. Our solution to this problem consists of our ability to impersonalize, and that means that regardless of who it may be that we think is ungrateful, unjust, immoral, or neglectful of us, this must be reversed instantly in the realization that to identify error with a person is to be guilty of malpractice, because it is seeing God's child as a sinner, as ungrateful, unlawful, unmerciful, instead of realizing God as the Selfhood of individual being, and thereby impersonalizing any erroneous appearance.

Eventually we include the entire world in our realization of God as individual being. We do not pin error on to any individual—not even ourselves. We do not claim that our jealousy, envy, greed, or lust is responsible for our ills because we do not have any such qualities. If temporarily those qualities may be expressing themselves through us, they must be recognized as

[7] Isaiah 2:22.

having their source in the impersonal carnal mind, and as long as they are out there, they are nothingness. This principle of impersonalization is one of the most important in our work, and we must make every effort to embody it in our consciousness because we will not find it expressed in our experience until we make it our own.

Watch what this secret of impersonalization does for you; watch what it does in the experience of those around you; and you will understand why the Master could say, "Love thy neighbor as thyself." [8]

Across the Desk

Please use the following as a meditation so frequently that never again will you forget it:

> *Regardless of what I think or believe, this does not change That which is. Regardless of what I may have faith in, this faith carries no power since the power is That which is, whether or not I have faith in It. There is really no power in my beliefs or my faith, since power exists whether or not I believe or have faith.*

To know that there is sky, earth, and sea requires no belief or faith. To know that apples come from apple trees or peaches from peach trees requires neither belief nor faith. To know that fish are in the sea, birds in the air, and that rain is wet requires neither belief nor faith.

Suppose that we do not believe these things or have faith in them, does that change anything? Does our lack of belief or lack of faith prevent the operation of nature's laws? So, no more does our lack of belief or lack of faith prevent the opera-

[8] Matthew 19:19.

tion of God's laws. To know that God is, is spiritual attainment. Not to know does not change the Is-ness of God.

Since God does not function in the human scene, no belief or faith in God will make It function there. For this reason, millions are praying to God, believing in God, and having faith in God, and receiving no answers to their prayers. God is not in the human scene. To bring God into our life and activity, it is necessary to *experience* God, and the knowing of the truth, becoming actually conscious of truth, and meditation—these help us to attain the experience of God.

Let us assume that we are faced with human problems that seem insurmountable. *There is a way out!* Relax. Rest. Let *My* Spirit be upon you. Let *My* peace be established within you. Let *My* grace take over the situation. There is an invisible Presence within you which will go before you as you withdraw thought and emotion and let the inner Invisible live and work through you.

When there are no problems, set aside time for daily meditations so that the weapons of the world do not prosper. Clothe yourself in *My* invisible robe. Let *My* light flow through you to human consciousness everywhere: friend and foe, near and far. Live *consciously* in *My* presence through *My* grace, and you will always experience *My* peace.

Is The Infinite Way Truth?

It is inevitable that occasions will arise which may cause you to question whether The Infinite Way is really truth. Many questioned the truth of Christianity even while the Master walked among them. Did not the disciples fall away at times? Lao-tze became so discouraged by the lack of recognition and acceptance that he just walked away from it all and disappeared.

This is to assure you that The Infinite Way *is* truth, but students—even practitioners or teachers—may at times fail. It is not the teaching that is power, but the measure of the student's *attainment* of the consciousness of Infinite Way truth. Only in proportion to our *attained* consciousness of truth are we the light that dispels the appearance of darkness. The principles of The Infinite Way will develop that consciousness in proportion to our study and meditation.

The Infinite Way is truth, and it cannot fail. Our devotion to the study and practice of its principles will enable us to attain the consciousness of truth, which reveals divine harmony where material evil or good appeared.

The object of The Infinite Way is not overcoming or destroying or rising above evil, but rather attaining that mind that was in Christ Jesus, or the Buddha-mind, which reveals the spiritual man and universe where evil or good humanhood has claimed existence.

Let us for a while forget about "doing good" or "saving the world" or "helping our fellow man" and give our entire attention to our own spiritual enlightenment until we are sought out. Be assured that as we attain a measure of realized Christhood the world will beat a pathway to us. Actually, we can benefit others only in proportion as we attain some measure of spiritual realization.

The multitudes came to the Master—he did not have to seek them. The multitudes still seek the Master. Be That, even in a degree, and the multitudes will seek you for the Light.

7) Unconditioned Infinity

It is an accepted part of natural normal human living for us to look outside ourselves to others for our good, for those things which we already have embodied within our own being. All of our years on earth, we have thought of ourselves as human beings, finite and limited, limited by our education, environment, or finances; and because we have so thought of ourselves, we have brought forth the demonstration of limitation. If, however, we had known that we are one with the Father, not two, and that all that the Father has is embodied within us, we would then know that what we call our Self is that divine son of God who has been given dominion over all that is, and to whom the Father has given His own allness.

Once we begin to realize that our real Self is not a personal limited self, a self limited to our personal sense of good, but rather that our Selfhood, our real being, is God, of which the human personality is but the outer form, or individual expression, then, through meditation, we learn to make contact with our divine Self. From the moment that we have contact with that divine Self, infinity begins to flow forth: immortality and eternality.

SELF-CONTAINED BEING

Because of our false education, we have accepted our human personality as our real self and have never looked within, but rather have looked outside, putting our faith in "princes":[1] in political preference, influence, or in the accident of birth. With the revelation of our true identity, we realize that the Self of us is God and, therefore, we can reach down into this Withinness and find ourselves one with the Vine, one with our divine Self-hood. The moment that contact is established, it is as if a voice said, "*I* am with you. *I* am going before you; *I* will be your bread, your meat, your wine; *I* will appear outwardly as your opportunity, as your companionship, as your home, as your safety, and as your security. *I* will do all things for you."

Now we no longer look to parents, children, neighbors, friends, brothers, or sisters. We look within ourselves, make contact, and then are patient until the flow begins to come from within, pouring forth as the without. After that, we do not have to depend on those outside us, but rather we can share with them out of this infinite Storehouse until they in their turn learn the infinite nature of their own being and begin to draw on it.

When the Master says, "If I go not away, the Comforter will not come unto you,"[2] he is indicating that we may draw on him until such time as we, too, have gained the realization that he gained, that is, that *I* in the midst of us is our wine, our water, and our bread, the Presence that appears in our experi-

[1] Psalm 146:3.
[2] John 16:7.

ence as divine harmony. We practice this by turning within each day, realizing that God within us is the Self of us, and it is our Father's good pleasure to give us the Kingdom. The Father knows what things we have need of even before we speak. Therefore, in this meditation we need only acknowledge:

> *Father, Thou art closer to me than breathing, even in the very midst of me, and because Thou art the infinite intelligence of this universe, Thou knowest my need even before I do. Before I could possibly ask, it is Thy good pleasure to give me the Kingdom, whatever that may be.*

> *It is Thy good pleasure to forgive me my sins; it is Thy good pleasure to go before me to "make the crooked places straight"* [3]*; it is Thy good pleasure to be my constant companion; it is Thy good pleasure to be my bread, my meat, my wine.*

> *Thou art my life eternal; Thou art my resurrection. Thou, Father, in the midst of me art my infinite supply, and only from the divine Fountain in the midst of me will I look for my good to flow.*

While we are doing this, we are "dying daily" to the belief that someone external to us must provide for us, that we are dependent on a person, a group, an employer, an investment, or upon anything except this infinite Self which is our being. This becomes easier for us when we think of ourselves in terms of capital "S" instead of small "s," think of ourselves as being the sons of God, heirs of God, and joint-heirs to all the heavenly riches.

Then we have impersonalized that self of ours, and gradually we come to realize that we are not finite being, we are not that creature who "is not subject to the law of God, neither

[3] Isaiah 45:2.

indeed can be," [4] for we now have the Spirit of God dwelling in us consciously, and this makes us the sons of God. If so be the consciousness of the presence of God be in us, then do we become the children of God, no longer mortal, no longer material, no longer finite, no longer dependent on any circumstance or condition external to our own being, but now dependent on our conscious union with God, our conscious oneness.

MIND IS NOT A CREATIVE AGENCY

When we struggle to demonstrate or create things for ourselves, usually those things that we want are already in existence, and probably belong to somebody else. Trying to draw them to ourselves, therefore, is like trying to draw unto ourselves the bread that somebody else has placed upon the waters.

The truth is that we do not need anything that belongs to anybody else: we do not need anybody else's money or his property. All we need is a conscious realization of God within us, unconditioned and free, and the supply comes to us without depriving anyone else of that which is his, and without lessening anyone else's supply. The correct interpretation of bringing spiritual supply into our experience is to bring it out of what might be called the Unmanifested, to bring it forth out of the Invisible. But to attempt to create with our minds is to draw to us that which is already in existence, that which is already finite, and in many cases already belongs to somebody else.

Using the mind for creative purposes always results in a state of limitation, because what we are demonstrating, then, is finiteness. If it were possible to demonstrate Infinity by some kind of mental manipulation, it would certainly be wise to use the mind to its fullest extent. But no one can create Infinity

[4] Romans 8:7.

with his mind because that would make a person greater than Infinity.

We cannot compress God within our mind; we cannot have a monopoly on God, not even a copyright; but we can become *aware* of the Infinity that is. The secret is to relax from mental activity and become aware of unconditioned Infinity. That we can do. We can become aware of God, and by becoming aware of the infinite nature of God, we bring into our experience all the forms necessary to our unfoldment.

NOT DRAWING TO OURSELVES BUT LIVING IN THE
CONSCIOUSNESS OF FULFILLMENT

When we open ourselves in the realization that our sufficiency is God's grace and that God's grace is not a thing, even though it appears visibly in our experience as a thing, we have the joy of knowing that whatever comes to us comes as the gift of God. It seems to come through others, but when it comes as the grace of God, it does not lessen that which others have, for God does not benefit one at the expense of another.

The materialistic view of life is that we need somebody else's money, land, or country; we need somebody else's this or we need somebody else's that. We do not. What we need is the grace of God; and in the recognition of that, we can have that Grace for It exists within our own being. "Son, thou art ever with me, and all that I have is thine." [5] Abide in that word, and then let supply flow. It does not always come from, or through, those from whom we may expect it. In fact, it rarely does.

As you well know, the economy of the United States has always prospered through the creation or discovery of things that did not exist yesterday: new materials, new methods, and new approaches to industrial and scientific problems. After World War I, the nation suffered a severe economic shock be-

5 Luke 15:31.

cause funds were no longer being channeled into war projects, and that resulted in the recession or depression of the early twenties. At that time, it was the development and phenomenal growth of the automobile industry, a comparatively new industry, that broke that depression within six months and set us on the way to prosperity again. So it has always been. This country has had successive periods of prosperity, not by acquiring what some other nation had, but by the spontaneous development of something new, something that came into expression without taking from others and which gave unto others out of a new-found abundance.

Once we, as individuals, come to the realization that we do not need anything that is already manifest in this world, we will not have to create anything. All we will have to do is open ourselves to Grace, and then an idea for a new product to be manufactured, a new talent, a new way of presenting something already in existence, or a new subject may be revealed to us. Always it will be a new something or other, expressing as the infinite flow of supply.

An excellent example of that principle can be found in the change that has taken place in the economy of Hawaii. For years and years, the prosperity of the Islands rested primarily upon increasing the production of sugar and pineapples, as if sugar and pineapples were the only basis for economic stability and well-being in that region. And what has happened to change that picture? Now Hawaii has discovered tourists! And aloha shirts, and mu-mus! With these new products, a whole new prosperity has blossomed.

So it is with us in our individual life. Let us realize that we do not need anything from one another. We should be glad to share with each other what we have, but we do not need anything from anyone because we have access to the kingdom of God within. When the Father reveals Himself, it is in infinite capacities, infinite quantities, infinite qualities—a whole infinity of good—and it is always in a way that is new or different, a way that is original, a way that adds to the world's good instead of taking from it.

If we could draw unto ourselves all the money in the world, we would have no pleasure in it because our heart would break, looking at the many without it. But it is a joyous experience to be able to increase the goods of this world, to be able to look at our particular world and feel that, in some small way, we have been responsible for bringing an increase of good into the whole world.

Is that not what industry, rightly understood, is doing today? Is it not bringing forth into expression the very good that we enjoy, and increasing the flow of supply in every direction? Industry is an activity that must be the human expression of God's grace, and often the bigger the industry, the better it is for all the world. Sometimes we are afraid of bigness, not realizing that if it were not for bigness, we would not have many of the things that we now have. Bigness does not take from the world: it gives to the world.

When a new idea springs into being, whether it is the automobile, the radio, television, or the airplane, be assured that somebody has touched cosmic consciousness and drawn out of it its secrets, and whenever that happens, mankind is going to be enriched.

In our present stage, there may be some evils connected with unrestricted industrial expansion because the world has not yet been brought to the place of brotherly love, of loving our neighbor as ourselves. We should be grateful, however, that we are living in an age when brotherly love is beginning to be practiced.

Let all of us rejoice when something new, spontaneous, and great comes into thought, whether it comes into your thought or mine, because it is adding to the whole. Let us not work with the idea of drawing to us from the world, but living in the consciousness of fulfillment.

THE SIGNIFICANCE OF THE INDIVIDUAL

You may believe that as long as you go your own sweet way, bothering no one, you are living your own life, and that nobody else is affected by it. You may think that you are unimportant, that you are unknown, or that you have no influence. That is the most disastrous state of thought that you can possibly entertain. There was no one more unimportant than Thomas Edison when he was selling newspapers on trains not long after the middle of the nineteenth century. But look what he accomplished! There was no one with less influence, money, or standing in the world in the early years when she was trying to establish Christian Science than Mary Baker Eddy. But think of what a blessing her work has been to the world!

Every person who has ever accomplished anything worthwhile has discovered that if he lives his life concerning himself with attaining wisdom for himself, he cannot keep it bottled up. It has to spread. There was no one more unimportant than Jesus Christ was as a Hebrew rabbi. But how true was his prophecy, "My words shall not pass away." [6] No, they never have, and they never will. They live on in consciousness awaiting our demonstration this very day.

There is no one, especially in a free world, who is really unimportant, nor is there anyone who can live solely and exclusively unto himself, even if he seems to be doing so. What is taking place in our consciousness is an influence, and therefore, if we are studying these principles for no reason other than to find out what is the secret of life, eventually they will do something to our life and eventually through us to someone

[6] Mark 13:31.

else's life. We have no way of knowing how widespread that may be in time.

There are unimportant people in this world, and they are all the people who believe they are unimportant, and that is what is keeping them unimportant. The truth is that you and I are important, and we are not only important to one another, but we are important to the entire world. We cannot fail to be a blessing to others if our attention is on seeking and searching out the secrets of life.

By this, I do not mean that everyone on earth should be a religious mystic or a spiritual healer. These spiritual principles will manifest themselves in new forms of music, new forms of art, new forms of literature, or new scientific discoveries. Never forget that. Our major responsibility is that we live by spiritual principles, and through the development of our spiritual awareness or Soul-faculties bring greater beauties and harmonies into this world than it has ever known.

It would be a sad commentary on the purpose of following the spiritual path to believe that we are dedicating our lives merely to making a few of us a little more comfortable in our bodies. Every healing serves as a witness to us that here is a principle of life which, when understood and practiced, will bring forth harmony—harmony of body, yes; harmony of mind, yes; harmony of purse, yes. But to go on from there to new forms—infinite forms of harmony and beauty and good will and peace—is the ultimate goal of the spiritual way of life.

THE BARRIER TO INDIVIDUAL FULFILLMENT

What is there in all the world that prevents us from being infinitely wise and infinitely loving? Nothing more nor less than this humanly mesmeric influence that was built around us when we were conceived, a mesmeric influence that begins to dissolve the moment that we recognize it for what it is and realize that it is not a power. True, it has acted as a power in our experience, but that is only because we have accepted the world belief in two powers, and now that we know there is but one power and that this nothingness is really nothing, we find that our consciousness is an inlet and an outlet for all the wisdom of God, for all the art, the literature, the music, the science —anything and everything which is our birthright.

Actually, it is not very likely that most of us will develop infinitely in more than one direction, but there have been those who have developed in four, five, and six directions. Such persons, and there have been many of them in the history of the world, are on the cosmic level. No hypnotism or mesmeric influence is operating in their minds to keep out God-wisdom, God-knowledge, and God-power, and thus they become a transparency through which art, science, literature, and many other worthwhile activities can flow.

Every person on earth would have supreme wisdom if this mesmeric belief in two powers did not keep it away from him. Without that belief, there is only the one infinite Consciousness manifesting Itself as individual consciousness.

As you practice the principle of one power and the two principles of impersonalization and "nothingization," you are lifted into a higher spiritual atmosphere in which you have contact with one another on the spiritual plane and with the wisdom of the world. Remember that God-consciousness is your individual consciousness, and therefore all that God is you are. All that God has is yours, "Son, thou art ever with me, and all that I have is thine." This "all" does not refer to money: it refers to life, wisdom, love, peace, joy, and dominion.

Watch the transformation that takes place in your own experience; watch the limitations that are broken down the moment you realize that there is nothing except this universal belief in two powers keeping you from being a transparency for

God, for the infinite nature of God, the infinite wisdom, life, love, and truth of God. This belief is not power, and it has operated heretofore only because, unknowingly and unconsciously, you have accepted the world belief. Only because of that has it functioned. But as you nullify any such false belief, it begins to lose its power in your life, and you become a greater transparency for divine wisdom, divine love, divine life, and divine power.

The divine Consciousness is the consciousness of every man and woman in the world, but that Consciousness cannot function through the mesmeric belief in two powers. It cannot function through selfishness because the nature of that Consciousness is an expressing consciousness, a giving and a bestowing one. The consciousness of God is a benediction to this world, continually flowing as a blessing. We have hindered its operation, not consciously, but because in our ignorance we have accepted self-preservation as the first law of nature. We have accepted two powers; we have accepted my mind and your mind, and then limited ourselves by how little or how much education we have, instead of realizing that God-consciousness knows no limitations. It embodies infinite wisdom, and It imparts it to all those who make of themselves a transparency for It.

BECOMING AN INSTRUMENT FOR THE DIVINE ACTIVITY

It is an impossibility for us to know *more* than God, and it is only possible for us to know *as much* as God if we have first reached that state of emptiness where we know nothing, and are then able because of that emptiness to let the wisdom of God manifest itself as our wisdom. By achieving a receptive attitude for the inflow, always maintaining a listening attitude, making of ourselves a vacuum, we wait for the new melody or new idea, the new vision, the new invention, or the new discovery to come to us.

When we learn to let both mind and body be the instruments for infinite Wisdom, which in silence and in stillness can manifest Itself as us, It performs Its functions through us. We cannot use God, but by attaining an inner stillness, God can use us, and It can manifest through us as healings if we have been chosen to be a part of the healing ministry, as inventions if we are inventors, or as music if we are composers.

God is infinity. All that is, is an emanation of God—whether it is to appear as engineering principles, scientific principles, literary works, art works, or whatever it may be—and we are the instruments through which and as which It is to function on earth. Our approach to life should be not one of learning how to use Truth, but how to be so receptive and responsive to the divine Impulse that Truth can use us, that Life can flow as our life, and Wisdom flow as our wisdom.

We open ourselves that we may be used by Truth, that God may manifest Itself as our individual being, that God may live Its life as us, that God may lead, guide, direct, govern, sustain, maintain, support, and supply, and that we may be the instruments through which or as which that takes place.

FINDING OUR NICHE IN LIFE

As we learn to turn within to that infinite Source, we, too, can draw out whatever it is that our particular nature needs for fulfillment. We do not all draw out the same thing. Because God is infinite, each person's nature is infinite. Some of us could not be fulfilled except through music or art, literature or truth, whereas others could not be fulfilled except through benevolence, invention, science, or construction. For each one, there is something that fulfills his nature, and by the ability to turn within to that Kingdom within his own consciousness, he draws forth from it that which is his fulfillment.

Ninety-nine percent of the people of the world are working for a living, and yet the work in which they are engaged is often not an activity that is fulfillment for them. Their work is something they merely tolerate, possibly because they began their careers before they knew enough about themselves. They started out young, got into the wrong kind of work for them, got married, had to support a family, and had no time, energy, or money to experiment until they found that which would have fulfilled them. So they had to stick with that with which they were stuck.

But with the understanding of the infinite nature of individual being, it is never too late because we can all turn within; we can all reach that infinite Source within ourselves and begin to draw forth our fulfillment. Then with patience we will find that we are moved one step at a time to that which is to be our life.

Unfortunately, most of those who come into metaphysics expect fulfillment to come the easy way, and it does not happen that way. Then, too, they may hesitate to embark on a new venture because they are afraid of that interval in between when they may seem to be a failure to the world, when they may not seem to be bringing forth fruitage. They expect to be led from where they are to their heavenly estate without the experiences that often do come when they have to give up the familiar ways they tried yesterday for the unknown ones of tomorrow. Often there are long bleak intervals between the old and the new, but with wisdom, they learn not to be afraid of failure; they learn not to be afraid of lack or limitation; they learn to be patient with their transitional experiences until they do come into their fulfillment.

Be assured of this: Our life's experience is the outpicturing of our own state of consciousness. Whatever limitations we are experiencing are the limitations of our state of consciousness, and they are going to continue until that state of consciousness develops and deepens and becomes enriched. Then the outer experience follows that new pattern.

There are times when we have a limited sense of ourselves, and then there are other times when for one reason or another that limited sense disappears and we are our natural selves. Or there may be times when we have a fearful sense, and for hours we may be walking around in fear or dread, and then all of a sudden it dissipates and is gone, and once again we are our normal natural selves.

Every sense of limitation, every sense of discord, every erroneous trait of character is nothing more than an erroneous sense that is gripping us, and the very moment that we begin to realize the one power and the nonpower of the mesmeric sense that heretofore we have accepted, a sense of freedom takes its place, and although we are the same person we were, nevertheless now we are free: "Whereas I was blind, now I see."[7] Whereas before we were under a sense of limitation, now we feel free. Whereas before we may have felt inadequate, now we feel adequate to whatever situation is brought into our experience. The whole thing really is a process of dehypnotization.

Many years ago, when I was devoting all my time to the practice of spiritual healing, I recognized as patients came to me how much they were functioning from an inner sense of limitation and how much they were governed by a sense of fear. Often I would hear associates of mine in the practice comment on this: "If so and so would only do this, or if so and so would only be this way, or if so and so would only overcome this!" Through observation, I saw that these inequities, injustices, and limitations were nothing more than this mesmeric sense, and then the question presented itself to me, "How do

[7] John 9:25.

you break this hypnotism? How do you break the hypnotism that is binding this person to greed, this one to miserliness, this one to lust, and this one to fear? How do you break this mesmeric sense?"

It required years of meditation and years almost of heartbreak before it was revealed to me that the way to break the hypnotism was to know that hypnotism is not power. That is the only way, and that has been the function of my work and the nature of my practice from that day to this—not trying to break hypnotism, not trying to free anyone from being hypnotized, but knowing that hypnotism itself is an activity of the carnal mind and therefore has no power and no law to sustain it, and that it is inoperative.

To be a transparency for infinite Intelligence and divine Love means to recognize that the carnal mind, this mesmeric influence of two powers, is not power, is not functioning in your or my experience, and has no law of God to maintain or sustain it.

The realization of these principles instantly begins to operate as a freeing influence in our consciousness. Such a realization does not heal us of anything; it does not enrich us; it does not improve our morals: it breaks the mesmeric sense and leaves us free to function as the spiritual and harmonious beings which we naturally are.

Across the Desk

Wanderlust has always kept me traveling. I have never been able to settle down in one place for very long, but always, after a brief pause, have felt that inner urge that has sent me forth seeking far places. In my human span, I have had five homes, and have never remained in one of them for more than a few weeks or a couple of months each year, and then pushed on, crossing many blue horizons. Even in these last ten years of living in beautiful Hawaii, I traveled thirty to thirty-five thousand miles a year before the jet age, and since then I have been traveling about sixty thousand miles a year.

I have found joy in travel, and peace of mind, and have shared happy hours with the wonderful souls I have met in so many different parts of the world. The goal of my travels has always been seeking some experience or understanding of the nature of the kingdom of God. The traveling was not undertaken because I expected to find the kingdom of God in some place, in some excitement or adventure, or in some country, but because I recognized the beauty of nights on the desert, days on great rivers and lakes, and the companionship of rare souls as a part of the journey to the Kingdom within.

While I have walked the main streets of the cities of North America, of London, Paris, Berlin, Vienna, and Rome, I have also experienced the desert of Egypt, the interior of the Belgian Congo, and the Zambezi River at Victoria Falls in South Africa. I have walked on the main streets of Sydney, Australia, and have had many happy hours in London Court in Perth on the west coast of Australia; and I have also been outside the cities where fantastic wood carving is still done with the most primitive of instruments.

But whether it has been in the midst of city traffic, in the quiet nights at sea, or traveling rivers and lakes, consciousness has always been centered within, even while enjoying the without. So peace is ever at hand, and yet a peaceful unrest that keeps one searching, traveling further afield, and traveling deeper within.

I was in the city of Roxbury, Massachusetts, on the night of the Roxbury fire, and witnessed the Spirit of God working in the many men and women toiling inside the fire area to rescue women and children having difficulty in getting out in time and helping the aged to get away from the danger of the flames. I have sat quietly with my friend, the old China hand, tucked away near the National Museum in London, and witnessed the Spirit of God as It lightened his eyes and brightened his face while he handled the rare treasures fashioned by the skilled hands of Chinese artists and carvers.

I have seen the devotion in the face of my Egyptian companion on my desert trips out of Cairo as he fingered his rosary and prayed, never less than five times every day, and often into the night, and I felt the very presence of God in him as he looked toward Mecca. I saw the very face of God in a stranger who came up to me on a Sunday in Hollywood, California, and asked why he felt an urge to make my acquaintance, and then found our common interest in the Bhagavad-Gita, of which he had made an excellent English translation. In that common bond of the love of Scripture, the grace of God flowed through this friendship for a long while.

At Elephanta off Bombay, India, while admiring the statuary in the caves and the wonders of that work, an Indian approached and invited me to lunch with him and his wife, and then wondered why he had been led to do this because it had never happened to him before. We did lunch together and formed a friendship which still lasts. His heart was reaching up to God, and when two or more of us were united by this common bond, he and his wife found their peace, and I, another experience of the activity of God on earth.

With a student, I spent a holiday at Victoria Falls in South Africa, and with him made a trip on the Zambezi River, and for several days experienced the joy of visiting that area. On the last day of our holiday, a couple spoke to the student who accompanied me and commented on the fact that they had observed us for several days and marveled at the wonderful relationship we had. They felt the peace and the understanding that existed between us, for they had noticed something of a nature never before known in two persons. It was true because there was a current of the Spirit of God constantly with us in every experience.

I have witnessed the selflessness of the Christ in the faces of the men at rescue work in the second flood of Galveston, Texas. As a guest at the first flight of the Zeppelin airship at Lake Constance in Switzerland, I saw the fire of devotion in the eyes of Count Zeppelin. On the street called Straight in Damascus, I felt the presence of God so strongly in the very midst of the crowds that thronged the street at noon that it seemed almost as if the very presence of St. Paul were at my side. At the castle in Edinburgh, Scotland, I was so overwhelmed with the Presence that for an entire day I experienced the joy of living entirely in the Spirit, and not only saw the beauty of the scenery, but was able also to see through the corporeal universe to the underlying incorporeality.

My wanderlust was not for the purpose of seeking God, but rather to find God everywhere, under every circumstance, from a peaceful, clear, moonlit night at the Taj Mahal to the soldier-filled streets of strife in Leopoldville in the Congo.

A young man who had made a good start in the business world, owing partly to his religious outlook on life, found himself "framed" into a prison sentence by his own father-in-law, a man of influence, and unable to prove his innocence or get the necessary legal representation that might have secured justice for him. When I met him in prison, his religious sense had completely evaporated, and he had lost all faith in God and in man, and for several weeks I found him difficult to approach. Finally, he consented to unite with me in prayer, only for the purpose of dwelling for a few minutes in the consciousness of God.

The following week, the judge who had tried and sentenced this man awakened out of a sleep with this man's name in his mind and, of course, with a troubled sense about it. The next day, he decided to look into the papers of that case to see why he was troubled, and he then found something in those papers that immediately caused him to bring about this man's release from prison, and eventually he was declared innocent. I was with this young man the day after he received notification of the judge's discovery of his innocence, and if ever the presence of God was on earth and reflected in a face, this was the time.

I have never known what many other men have found in life in the experience of marriage, family, home, and business, but I have found the presence of God, the love of God, the light of God in people, in places, in things. I have found joy in my wanderlust, and I suppose I will continue as long as I catch glimpses of God's grace, God's touch, and can witness His Spirit on earth as It is in heaven. I do not seek the kingdom of God, but the experience of God, here, there, and everywhere, and continue on into the Invisible, where, even if I make my bed in hell, His presence will reveal Itself there.

8) On the Sea
of Spirit

Life on the spiritual path can be divided into three major periods: the first a very pleasant one, the second not quite so comfortable, and the third not only pleasant but satisfying. The first stage is pleasant because our thoughts are centered primarily on changing conditions of evil, error, discord, and inharmony into more harmonious conditions, and, as many of us have discovered, some of these changes do take place. We gain a better sense of health, very often a much better sense of supply, and our human relationships adjust themselves and become much more satisfactory than they were before. In this first stage of our spiritual unfoldment, it is a joyous thing to watch some part of the old man "die," [1] and the new man be "born," watch the old conditions disappear, and new and more harmonious ones appear.

[1] I Corinthians 15:31.

LIVING IN TWO WORLDS

The second stage is probably the longest period, and the most difficult one. This is because in the second stage we are living in two worlds. We have glimpsed something of the nature of Reality, and something of the unreal nature of the phenomenal world, gradually leading us to a state of consciousness where we do not quickly run for an aspirin the moment we have a cold, or immediately consult a doctor when something more serious develops. We have little or no fear about these disturbing physical conditions because they no longer hold the same terror for us. Unfortunately, most of our friends do not think as we do, and they can make life fairly miserable for us by reminding us that we must be practical, that we must protect ourselves from disease and danger, and that it is unreasonable and impractical to forgive our enemies.

Because of this conflict, we often find ourselves living in two worlds with the necessity of catering to both of them. Apparently, there is no way of running away from either one of them; and inasmuch as we do not want to lose the spiritual ground that we have gained by so much work, study, and meditation, we have no choice but to live temporarily in these two worlds. That means that we may sometimes be called upon to take medicine, or to commiserate with our friends and relatives even when we do not agree with what they are doing. Outwardly, we have to be in this world—even though not of it—be as loving as possible, when as a matter of fact we are not too patient with all that goes on about us. But we cannot let anyone see our impatience, because that would not be loving. So we sometimes engage in double-talk. We say things that we really do not believe, and do things of which we do not in our hearts approve.

When I was in training in World War I, I went through a period of bayonet lessons with a major who was very famous for his training of Marines and who taught us to say with every lunge we made, "You filthy Hun! You so and so, and so and so, and so and so!" All the time I was supposed to be doing that, I was inwardly forgiving my enemies and loving them. It is not easy to live a double life, but there are times when we have to do it.

This second period in our development is difficult, also, because we are not yet firmly grounded in the truth. We do not yet have the full conviction that all the things we have learned are true. Yes, it says so in the books, and yes, so and so says so, and yes, we believe it, but—but—. So here we are trying to hold firmly to something we have not yet completely demonstrated.

WHEN PROBLEMS BECOME OPPORTUNITIES

Once we get past the second stage, which may be anywhere from our second to twenty-second year of study, we begin to enjoy life because now we are so completely removed from the hates and the fears of this world and from any doubts of the principles we may have had that we can live this double life without any reaction to ourselves. There is then no inner conflict when we speak in the language of the day because, within ourselves, we are living in the consciousness we have now attained. As a matter of fact, much more is demanded of us in this third stage because others begin to seek us out for help, but every problem that is brought to us is just another opportunity for the living of the consciousness that we have attained, and at this state of consciousness it does not strike us as a problem.

In the first stage and somewhat in the second, every time a problem presented itself, we usually rebelled, "Why did that have to come to me? I have been so serious in my study; I have been so faithful. Now, why did this come to me?" So we were waging a battle with ourselves. In this third stage, however, we know that the higher we go, the more problems will be presented to us, only now they are not exclusively our personal problems: they are the problems of the world—friends, family, patients, students. These bring the problems, but to us they are no longer problems. Now they are opportunities.

When we gain an understanding of this, there will come long periods of conversation with ourselves in which we try to make it clear to ourselves that if we have temptations that do not seem to yield immediately, we will realize that no demonstration can rise higher than the consciousness from which it emanates. We say, "Ah, yes, I have God-consciousness." Indeed we have, but that is not the consciousness that is governing our daily life—not yet! It is when we come to the third stage that we are God-governed. In the first stage, we are hoping to be God-governed; in the second stage, we are beginning to see some fruitage in the spiritual life; but it is only in the third stage where we really become the child of God, an heir, and live by Grace.

CONSCIOUSNESS, THE DETERMINING FACTOR

Let us see how this works out, so that we do not lose patience with ourselves, so that we understand that we really do have a work ahead of us which must be grounded on principles, and not just on blind faith. I, myself, am infinite divine Consciousness. This is just as true of you as it is of me, so you can repeat to yourself: "I, myself, am infinite divine Consciousness." However, I still see a great deal of the "natural man" [2] in me, and to that extent, I am not wholly governed by divine Consciousness: I am governed partly by divine Consciousness and partly by the man-whose-breath-is-in-his-nostrils consciousness.

As human beings, we are not under the law of God, the grace of God, or under the protection of God; and therefore, in those first few months when we begin our study, 99 per cent of

[2] I Corinthians 2:14.

the time we are living under the carnal mind; yet at the same time we are benefiting by the more advanced consciousness of those who are guiding us in our spiritual unfoldment. In those early months, however, our consciousness is not sufficiently advanced for us to take full advantage of the help given us by those who have gone further on the Path.

Proof of this truth is found when we observe children of a beautiful mother or a handsome father, or both. They nearly always reflect the consciousness of their parents, and so the beauty and integrity of the parents' consciousness can usually be seen in the face and body of the child. When that child becomes sixteen, seventeen, eighteen, or nineteen, however, he begins to live his own life and to manifest his own consciousness. How often does that beautiful child become an ugly duckling! On the other hand, how many children who have been ugly ducklings, when under their parents' consciousness, become beautiful once they begin to reflect their own state of consciousness, which sometimes is far more beautiful than that of their parents.

If parents maintain their spiritual consciousness and live in the realization of one power, the child of spiritually endowed parents can be expected to be 80 per cent free of children's diseases, of delinquent behavior, of accidents, and of the fears that normally beset children. If, however, that child does not accept some of the principles by which his parents have been able to give him that immunity during his childhood years, he is more than likely to lose the benefit of his parents' consciousness once he is living through his own consciousness and has come out from under the umbrella of the parents' consciousness.

So, too, as students, we are benefiting by the consciousness of our teacher. We are experiencing far less of the world's discords and inharmonies because the consciousness of our teacher is acting as the law unto our experience. If we, ourselves, are not learning these principles, however, practicing meditation and developing our own consciousness, then when the teacher goes away, the Comforter is found to be no longer with us.

LIVING WITH THE PRINCIPLES

In these early days, we are gaining an understanding of the principles: learning to pray aright, learning to meditate, learning to live in the consciousness of one power, and learning to live in an awareness of Omnipresence, Omnipotence, Omniscience. Year by year, there is less of the "natural man" about us, and more and more of that mind which was also in Christ Jesus. So it is that we go through all our student-days partly under the law and grace of God, and partly under the law of the "natural man." When problems come, then, they represent that degree of the "natural man" which has not yet been overcome. Not a single one of us can hope to be completely transformed into the Christ by a few years of study. That cannot happen! But, in proportion to our study and meditation, we do manifest less and less of the "natural man" and demonstrate more and more of the divine Consciousness.

As long as we have not yet fully overcome the "natural man," which is "not subject to the law of God, neither indeed can be," [3] we cannot receive the things of God. As problems arise, therefore, what we are called upon to do is to remember that this "natural man" is not of God, is not a power, a presence, or a reality. The purpose of the spiritual life we are trying to lead is to recognize the carnal mind every time it raises its head: "I know thee who thou art. Get thee behind me! Thou art not of God; therefore, there is no reality to you; there is no spiritual law or divine grace to support, maintain, or sustain you." The degree in which the son of God has been raised up

[3] Romans 8:7.

in us is the measure in which we can turn on the carnal mind with its manifestations, and nullify it.

It is important that students catch well the principles of impersonalization and "nothingization," so that in the event that problems come to them, they do not say, "How could that happen to me? I have been reading the books all year. I have been meditating all year."

It is not the amount of reading and meditating that counts. What counts is what degree of Christ is raised up in students, what degree of loving their neighbors have they accomplished, what degree of forgiving their enemies, what degree of resisting not evil, what degree of realization of one power. This determines the degree of their freedom from discord, and it determines the nature of their ability to meet problems quickly and decisively.

IMPERSONALIZE FAILURE

Some may think that faith plays a part in this, but faith does not enter into this in any way whatsoever. It is not a matter of having faith: it is a matter of actually understanding these principles and having the ability to apply them impersonally, not merely when everything is going well, but when the "chips" are down. When we are faced with that Satan, that condition, we must be able to stand fast and say, "Aha! This is the universal belief in two powers."

Another temptation that comes is the tendency to blame ourselves for something we have done. When we do this, we are not impersonalizing. Once we say, "Oh, I am at fault. I guess I am not a good student. Evidently I do not understand. Others do, but I don't," we are personalizing, and as long as we personalize, we have fallen overboard. We have fallen into the trap, and we are going to have a struggle.

Let us do as Paul did, not claim to have fully arrived, but to "press toward the mark for the prize of the high calling of God in Christ Jesus." [4] Let us recognize, "I am not looking at the past; I am going forward. I do not claim to have attained Christhood. I claim only that Christhood is my true identity, and that as I come into the realization of my Christhood, in that degree I am God-governed, and there can be no problems, certainly none of my own."

Then, when temptation in the form of a problem comes, we will remember that we are not dealing with any failure on our part: we are dealing with the appearance of a universal claim of two powers, with the claim of personalized evil or discord, and it is up to us to put our heel on it.

Whereas we may not be responsible for being ninety years of age, we are responsible for being old at ninety years of age. That is a universal claim. In fact, at seventy and at eighty, age is a universal claim, and if we are going to accept the universal claim as being personal to us, then we are the ones that manifest it. We must understand that in our true identity, the *I* of us is as old as God and as young as God, because *I* coexists with God. I have no more beginning than God has a beginning, and I have no more ending than God has an ending. This, you know, and I know. Ah, yes! We all know it—until we get a twinge of rheumatism, and then somebody reminds us that we are forty-eight or eighty-four.

In dealing with any problem, we impersonalize the entire picture, and once we have impersonalized it, the problem has no person in whom, on whom, or through whom to operate. In other words, we must lay the ax at the root of the tree. Every time that we give way to doubt or discouragement, it is because we are personalizing the universal belief in two powers, and holding ourselves responsible for it.

The life of the Spirit demands much of all of us. The Master

4 Philippians 3:14.

said, "Strait is the gate, and narrow is the way, which leadeth unto life, and few there be that find it." [5] And perhaps the reason so few enter is because the spiritual path demands that we stand fast on certain principles, and one of the major principles is impersonalization.

It is undoubtedly true that as long as there is belief in two powers, a belief in good and evil in the world, people are going to act in a good or an evil way. But if we continue condemning our friends and our neighbors, we have no way to enter the higher consciousness, and we will experience good and evil until such time as we actually realize that we have no right to be functioning as human beings, to have human feelings of good or evil, and certainly no right to have human will.

LIVING IN THE HIGHER CONSCIOUSNESS

Once we begin to understand the true nature of our identity and know our secret name, we then come into a whole new mode of life. We rely now on that hidden manna which is our divine Consciousness:

> *My real Consciousness, that Consciousness which God gave me, is my hidden manna. It is from this Consciousness that my life emanates: my prosperity, my friendships, my judgments, my guidance, my art—everything that pertains to my life.*

Up to a certain point, we are not proving this. What we are experiencing is a combination of good and evil: some aspects of our life are good and some bad; some up and some down; some rich and some poor. This is because we are functioning on the level of the belief in good and evil. But when we attain this higher consciousness, we recognize, "Ah, but that was in the days of my ignorance, when I thought I was man, when I

[5] Matthew 7:14.

thought I had no control over this world or that I was not at-one with God and under the law of God. But now, now I know my secret name."

I am the son of God; I am an heir of God, joint-heir: the word I makes me so. I will never leave me, nor forsake me. I, the Christ, will be with me to the end of the world. Therefore, I am spiritual consciousness; I am immortal: I was never born, and I will never die. I live, and move, and have my being in God, and God in me, for we are one.

This conscious awareness that "I and my Father are one," [6] *that I and the infinite divine Consciousness are one—this is my hidden manna.*

This divine Consciousness, which I am, is the substance of all form. It is the substance of my tomorrow—the hours and the minutes of my tomorrow, the dollars, the food, the rela- tionships, the clothing, the transportation, the activity, and the success of all my tomorrows. I of my own self can be nothing, but the I that I am, which I now recognize to be my Christ- Selfhood, this is my hidden manna.

Such a recognition deprives us of the privilege and the lux- ury of having desires. We have no right to have desires: we must now be beholders, letting God's grace flow from our con- sciousness. We have no right to have a will of our own; we must live always at the standpoint of being beholders, bearing witness to God's will being manifest through us. We have no right to know lack, limitation, or unhappiness because we are watching the infinite Spirit of God flow forth from us, through us, and as us. We are beholders. We lose the privilege of hav- ing fears or doubts, or of losing hope, because if we indulge in those temptations we are taken back to our mortal selfhood, the one that is supposed to be "dying," or already "dead."

6 John 10:30.

In the degree, then, that we have human desires, human will, human ambition, human fears, and human doubts, in that degree are we denying and crucifying our Christhood.

THE HIDDEN MANNA

Instead of indulging in such humanhood, we must cherish, deep within us, our hidden manna:

I have hidden manna. My hidden manna is the divine Consciousness which I am. It is the fullness of the Godhead bodily. In Its presence is fulfillment. It can give me spiritual peace, harmony, rest, completeness, perfection, guidance, wisdom, and direction.

This is my hidden manna, and no one in the world—not even my mother—can see it! No one can see the divine Consciousness which I am, nor can he see my awareness of It because I do not go out in the street and talk about It. Secretly and sacredly, I realize within myself, "Thank You, Father, that I have learned that God constitutes my being."

My hidden manna is that awareness; and therefore, infinity is the measure of my demonstration; immortality is the measure of my life. Nothing else! There is no big or little; there is no great or small; there is no up or down: there is just Allness.

God is the substance of my days, and God is the substance of my nights, and everything that flows into my days and my nights is God-action, God-activity, God-substance, God-presence, God-law. This is my hidden manna, and I can rest and relax in it.

This realization is like resting back upon a cloud, floating on a Sea of Infinity, living, moving, and having our being in this divine Grace, and letting It flow—doing nothing, taking no thought for the morrow. Each moment of every day or night, we do those things that are given us to do without anxiety, without fear, without doubt. Why? Because permeating our being is divine Wisdom, divine Energy, divine Love, immortal Life, immortal Spirit!

Unless we are able to rest back and float on that Sea of Infinity, we have no conscious awareness of our hidden manna. When we can do that, it is because we have realized that "greater is he that is in [us] than he that is in the world." [7] This conviction is the understanding that, because God constitutes our being, God is the essence and substance of our life, that in the presence of our very own consciousness there is rest, quiet, contentment, peace.

"In quietness and in confidence," [8] *I rest, knowing that I have this hidden manna, that God constitutes my consciousness, that God constitutes my todays and my tomorrows.*

TIME IS ALWAYS NOW

We may break tomorrow into hours, minutes, and seconds, but what is the substance of an hour, a minute, or a second? Can we separate time from God? Can we have time somewhere and God somewhere else, or is God the essence and substance of all the time there is?

The clock is what would divide infinity into periods called hours and days. But if we remove the clock from our thought, we will soon see that there are no days, hours, or minutes: there is just an infinite and an eternal now, a now that is going on, and going on, and going on—always being now; it is never being afterward, it is never being before, it is always being now. The calendar divides time into weeks, months, and years,

7 I John 4:4.
8 Isaiah 30:15.

but all we have to do is see how many times the calendar has been changed, and realize that it may be changed again, to know that there is no such thing, really, in the kingdom of God, as a division of time. When we remove the clocks and the calendars from our consciousness, we see that we are here in this space, in this time, and that space is always *here* and that time is always *now,* and in each period of our nowness, we have a function to perform.

God is the substance of our time; God is the substance of our days; God is the substance, the activity, and the law of our nights, and that is why there is no age: there is only now.

> God is the substance, the law, and the activity of my consciousness. God is the activity of my time; God is the substance of my tomorrows. Now I am in God's time; now I am in God's care; now I am floating back on that Sea of Spirit, that Ocean of Contentment.

This contentment I have often felt as a cloud around my shoulders, as if I were resting back on this cloud, this cloud of Spirit, of peace, of rest.

LIFTING UP THE *I*

As we dwell in the awareness of our divine Consciousness, the "natural man" of us is "dying." Why is it "dying"? It is fed only by our thoughts, and when our human life, our carnal selfhood, is not in our thoughts, it is "dying." The more we live in the conscious awareness of God as constituting our being, the more the "natural man" is being lessened, until finally it fades away entirely.

We maintain and sustain the evils, the errors, and discords of our life by thinking about them, but as soon as we no longer think about them, they cease to be because they never existed at all outside our thinking. As we stop dwelling on our triumphs and our failures, they no longer exist. Instead, Christ lives our life.

How are we going to demonstrate the truth that the Christ lives our life? How are we going to demonstrate that we can do all things through the Christ? The first step is to give up the personal pronoun "I": "I" fear; "I" doubt; "I" am not able; "I" do not have the ability; "I" do not have the time. That personal sense of "I" must be given up, and we must remember that our hidden manna is our awareness of this indwelling Christ.

As long as we abide in the awareness of our indwelling Christ, the things of "this world" [9] must lessen and lessen and lessen until they disappear. The longer we carry around in our thought the fears of "this world" the less chance we have of losing them. They must be dropped first! They cannot be dropped psychologically—that has been tried. We cannot psychologize ourselves out of our fears. There is only one way in which we can drop the concerns of the human world, and that is to let the Christ fill our consciousness, to have the constant awareness of this hidden manna: "I live; yet not I, but Christ liveth in me." [10] We cannot live up there with that, and hate or fear something down here. The Christ is come to our consciousness that we might have life, and that we might have it more abundantly. But it is our conscious awareness of this that brings it to our experience.

We must know that we have this hidden manna, and what it is. We cannot have a blind faith that it is a something-or-other. It is not a charm: it is the understanding that God is our consciousness, that the Christ is our mind, that the Christ is the law that operates through us. This is our hidden manna. This

[9] John 18:36.
[10] Galatians 2:20.

is the secret we cannot tell the world because we would be crucified for it, as others have been before us. It will not be crucifixion on a cross, but we will be crucified in our Soul by being laughed at and ridiculed. So, we must keep this locked up in our consciousness, and, when the world sees the practicality of this way of life, sees the harmonious lives that unfold, there will be no argument or criticism left. Be still; be still about this hidden manna. Then, even if the world does not believe, there will be no argument left.

Everything about our human world—its customs, language, and mode of operation—makes life difficult for us as we try to hold steadfast and maintain this Word in our consciousness. The difficulty is that we pay lip service to the conversation of the world, and at the same time always have to maintain our own spiritual integrity within, and yet not voice it without.

That is why it is imperative to have many periods of ten, twenty, or thirty seconds or minutes for pausing in the midst of the day or night to relax, to remember, and to float back on the Sea of Spirit. That is why it is so essential to close our eyes at times to sense testimony, and remember, "Thank You, Father. *I* in the midst of me is my hidden manna."

All this time we are lifting up the *I* in us, lifting It from the personal sense of "I" to the *I* that we really are. We are crucifying that personal sense of "I," and if we keep it up long enough it will be "dead," and there will be nothing left but the *I* that we are, and with it *My* peace and *My* grace, *My* wholeness, *My* completeness, *My* harmony, *My* justice.

We have to remember often that the Christ-Self is our true identity, whereas the "natural man" is that part of us which was imposed upon us at birth and to which we are now "dying." To the degree in which we lift up the *I* in us, are we "dying daily" to the personal sense of "I." In the degree that we take no thought, but rest in the Sea of Spirit, are we letting the

Christ live our life, and then each moment of the day we do those things given us to do.

An understanding student will not believe that this way is a way of doing nothing. In one sense, it is; but this "doing nothing" makes us lead a very busy life because the "doing nothing" is not really a doing nothing; it is doing nothing of a personal nature. It is doing nothing through personal fear or personal doubt; it is doing nothing that is purely of our will or our desire. In this sense, it is doing nothing, but it really is a very active existence because God is fulfilling Himself as our individual experience.

IMMORTALITY REVEALED

God is fulfilling Himself and His destiny as our individual experience. This is not your life or my life to do with as we would like: this is God's life which God is living as us. Once we begin to perceive this, we will understand immortality.

We cannot understand immortality while we think of our life as being ours because we know right well that that personal sense of life comes to an end, and, as long as we hold to that belief, we can have no sense of immortality. There is no way of perpetuating eternally a limited sense of self. Instead we must "die daily" to that limited sense of self and realize, "It is not my life that is eternal: it is the God-life which is living Itself as my life that is eternal." God-life cannot die; It cannot age; It cannot be diseased. The more we realize that this is God-life, that this is God-consciousness appearing as us, the more we lose concern for our own life in the realization that God knows how to maintain and sustain His life, which is ours.

Knowing our true identity is the hidden manna. It is the ability to rest back, knowing that God has no limitations whatsoever, and that God lives our life. God cannot die; God cannot sin; God cannot be sick.

Christ is the eternal son of God, which was never born and will never die; and that Christ, the divine son of God, lives as my eternal life.

Let us relax and rest in this truth. Let this be our "meat" that the world knows not of, but which we know and understand. This is our secret meat, our spiritual meat, the substance of our life, the understanding of our true identity, the understanding of our Christ-life, of our Christ-mind, of our Christ-Soul, of our Christ-being.

But what about all the sins of which we have been guilty? We never were! This is only personal sense, the "natural man," which is the cloak, the mask. *Persona,* mask! Our personality is a mask that we have been wearing. As we strip off the personality, there is no more mask, and we stand revealed in our true Christ-identity.

Across the Desk

The Chicago work given last month[11] was certainly of a unique nature in every way. My class work followed naturally the work in Portland and Seattle and gave us some new working principles, or at least new approaches to the living and practice of The Infinite Way.

Tonight, June 5,[12] I completed a six-session Manchester Closed Class on scriptural meditations, a class to end all classes on meditation as taught and practiced in The Infinite Way. Put this class, which has been recorded on three tapes, on your memorandum to order when you are ready. You will find it important. I know because I watched a miracle unfold as this message came through.

[11] May 1964.
[12] June 1964.

There is a secret known to the few which must eventually be known and understood and practiced by all. Peace can be established on earth by one, but more swiftly by two or more, and very quickly by "ten" [13] righteous men. This you may prove first in your family, business, professional, and community life. Once you have succeeded, it will not be necessary to ask you to encompass the universe because you will no longer have the power to refrain from doing so.

Set aside one meditation period each day—and a few minutes each time will be sufficient—to sit in meditation with the inner ear opened. That is all: no praying, no asking, no seeking, especially no desires to be fulfilled. Just meditate with the inner ear open, and then go about your business. Give a specific period to this each day, and do not let yourself watch for results. In due time, fruitage will appear in some form of harmony within yourself, your home, your family, or your business, art, or profession.

As fruitage appears, raise your consciousness to take in the weather, elections, national and international relationships. Remember that none of these subjects enters your thought while in meditation. You may not even think of peace on earth. Just be still. Listen with the invisible ear for the inaudible Word. You are thus ushering in the kingdom of God on earth as it is in heaven.

[13] Genesis 18:32.

9) The Revelation of Spiritual Identity

The only reason the subject of spiritual healing is emphasized in our work is that the practice of this kind of healing deepens and enriches consciousness, and through this practice, the everyday problems of life touch us in a decidedly minor degree. But healing work is not the end or the object of our being on the spiritual path. Rather is it incidental to the major goal of attaining God-realization.

Anyone who has had any experience in metaphysics must have observed that the life ambition of far too many students is to become either healthy or prosperous, but, at some time or other, these students must learn that lack is not as great a problem as it has been painted, nor is illness. In fact, both disease and lack may serve as incentives to drive us out of the physical and mental limitations with which we have bound ourselves. These limitations are brought about not because the mind and the body are evil or sick, but only because both mind and body have been conditioned by the belief in two powers.

A mistake often made by students in their practice of spiritual healing, and one which has been pointed out in previous chapters, is to treat effects—headaches, storms, cancers, polio—denying them or in some way trying to handle them. Never make that mistake. Never under any circumstance treat heart disease, tuberculosis, or any disease of which you have ever heard, or any accident. These are only effects. If you could remove every one of them, the cause would still be there, and the cause is a belief in two powers, a belief in the carnal mind.

If, at this moment, you could be made whole, nothing would stop you from becoming sick or poor again tomorrow, unless you, yourself, had come to the realization that the healing that had taken place was not one of lack or limitation, of fear, of sin or false appetites, of polio, cancer, blindness, or deafness: the healing was in being freed from the belief in two powers—good and evil.

Once you begin to heal on this basis, you will find that those who come to you for help are given years and years of freedom from the everyday discords and inharmonies of life. You have set them free—not from their ills, but from the *cause* of their ills, the universal belief in good powers and bad powers.

If you are dealing with a cold or the flu, be willing quietly to ponder, reflect, meditate, and cogitate on this truth:

God, infinite Being, besides which there is no other! God, Omnipotence! There is no other power. Nothing can be empowered to do evil. How could it be if God is infinite, if God in infinite good and infinite omnipotence? God constitutes all being.

What I am faced with is not evil. It is not a destructive germ. I am faced with a belief in two powers, and I do not accept it. There cannot be God and any other power. There cannot even be a power for good anywhere: there can be only God Itself maintaining and sustaining the integrity of Its own being.

After you have watched the cold or the flu dissolve a few times, you begin to have less faith in the power of evil and much more confidence in the principle of oneness and assurance that this is the great principle of life.

ALL EVIL, A UNIVERSAL MALPRACTICE

The idea of power always suggests one power doing something to another power, and that is why we have to be thoroughly saturated with the principle of nonpower. Then, we do not even want a God-power to do something for us. We are satisfied that God in Its infinite power and wisdom is already doing all that God is supposed to do. Therefore, we need never call upon God or God's power to do anything. So we get used to the idea of not turning to a God-power, or the power of truth over error, or good over evil, or God over devil. Our whole consciousness is built on the realization of God constituting all being, and therefore there is neither good nor evil. There is only God.

If you can accept God as the creative, maintaining, and sustaining Principle of life, if you can accept the fact that this is a God-created universe and not an accidental one, then you must be able to accept the fact that negative or evil power cannot have any existence outside the mind that believes in it.

But because the mind that believes in evil power is the universal mind, every human being to some extent accepts negative or evil powers. Therefore, begin individually to live and move and have your being in the realization of God, and then realize that all else is nothing but mental malpractice, a belief in two powers. Instead of treating disease as disease, sin as sin, or lack as lack, treat it as malpractice, a belief in two powers; and instead of fearing it as malpractice and saying, "Oh, but I must protect myself from malpractice," realize the nature of malpractice as the activity of the human mind, and therefore a nothingness.

All evil—whether it appears as lack or limitation, as destructive weather, as infection or contagion, or even epidemics—is malpractice, but it is not the directed thought of an individual: it is the universal malpractice which arises out of the belief in two powers. Your protection is to live in one power, being convinced that anything other than the presence of God is not power. That is your protection, and then none of the evils of the world can enter to defile or make a lie within you.

Basic to effective healing must be the realization that you are not dealing with disease or sin; you are not dealing with floods, tidal waves, or typhoons: you are dealing with a universal malpractice made up of the belief in two powers. The water that you see as a mirage on the desert is not water: it is malpractice, and that malpractice is making you see something that does not exist; it is throwing a picture at you and making you see it erroneously. With that realization, watch how quickly the error begins to subside and then finally dissolve.

If you have been a student of some metaphysical teachings, you may have been made to fear people and their malpractice, but now release yourself from that nonsense. It makes no difference if there are persons so misguided as to attempt to malpractice: they are not malpractitioners, and you need fear nothing from them. They are themselves victims of malpractice, of this universal belief in two powers.

You can quickly deprive them of that power just as you can deprive a hypnotist of his power. A hypnotist, trying to hypnotize some person or even a whole group of persons, cannot succeed if there is one individual who knows the one Power. The minute someone knows that the human mind, that is, the belief in two powers, is not power, and that this belief that mind is power is just the "arm of flesh,"[1] or nothingness, the hypnotist is ineffective.

RECOGNIZE ANY PROBLEM AS ANTI-CHRIST

There is another term, which is equally effective in healing work, and that is anti-Christ. When faced with any problem, recognize it as anti-Christ. In other words, this evil is not aimed at you: it is aimed at the Christ of you.[2] Nobody dislikes or hates you enough to want to make you sick or cause you to die, but this universal malpractice would, if it had intelligence enough, try to wipe out your Christhood.

The Master exemplified the truth revealed throughout all time that wherever the Christ appears, It is crucified. The Christ has always been crucified, and the Christ will always be crucified; but is is not a nation or a race that will crucify It: it is the universal belief in two powers that is the anti-Christ to you and to me.

Therefore, when something like a calendar on the wall says, "You are past threescore years and ten," just look at it and say "Anti-Christ! You, hanging up there on that wall, you do not have any power over me!" Imagine giving power to a calendar on a wall! And yet does it not frighten every one of us because of what we have accepted as the belief about the calendar?

It makes no difference whether it is a simple cold, an epidemic of polio, or a cancer, please try to remember this: You are not dealing with names; you are not dealing with effects: you are dealing with the only cause of discord that has ever existed in the world, and that is the hypnotism that comes out of the belief in two powers. Whether you call it hypnotism, anti-Christ, or malpractice, as long as you impersonalize it and

[1] II Chronicles 32:8.
[2] For a complete discussion of this subject, see Chapter Six.

recognize that, because of the nature of God, it must be impotent, you are free—or at least you are on your way to freedom. You will attain your complete freedom in proportion to your ability to impersonalize every phase of error and then negate it by resting in the Word—by "nothingizing" it. Do not go out to battle an enemy that is stronger than you are because you will be overcome by your belief that it is power, and every attempt you make to fight it makes it more powerful.

That is why it is not always wise for practitioners to make personal calls on patients. Very, very seldom do I do that—so seldom that I cannot even remember the last time. Why should I? To get the water off the road? It was not there to begin with. So why should I go there to try to remove it from the road? Is there a power to be fought? No, there was no power to begin with, and my running around would merely represent my own degree of fear. Therefore, the wisest course for me to pursue is to stay right at home and realize its nothingness.

Evil is not evil: it is anti-Christ, and anti-Christ is not power. Anti-Christ must be recognized as a nothingness, a nothingness that would, if it could, destroy spiritual existence. But can immortality be destroyed? Can eternality be destroyed? Can Omnipotence have an opponent?

When you translate sin, disease, death, lack, or limitation into such words as "Oh, this is malpractice, a belief in two powers," or "This is anti-Christ, a belief in two powers," or "This is a universal hypnotism, a belief in two powers," you have every right to drop it, turn right over and go to sleep, instead of sitting up, fearing it, fighting it, and protecting yourself from it, when in reality there is no "it."

There is no difference between one disease and another. There is no difference between one sin and another. It is only a matter of realizing that the water on the desert is not water, but a mirage, that disease is not disease, lack is not lack, limitation is not limitation, hate is not hate, hypnotism is not hypnotism. All this is mirage. Rest in the Word, and do not go out to fight the enemy.

GOOD IS OMNIPRESENT

For more years than I care to tell you about, the thought plagued me: How can I love God? I didn't have a trace of feeling in my soul, my mind, or my heart for God, and I did not know how to love God. I could love God only when I realized that God is not responsible in any way, shape, or manner for the evils of the world, nor is there anything God can do about our false beliefs. I could love God then because I saw the impotence of so-called evil powers. Now I can love God with all my heart and with all my soul, for I know God is maintaining and sustaining His universe.

Once it is recognized that the so-called powers of this world are not powers, it will not be long before heaven is established on earth. There is only one power. The belief in two powers which constitutes the carnal mind is temporal power, and it operates as mental and physical power only as long as the belief exists. Once you come, even in a measure, to the realization of God—no good powers, no bad powers, only God, and only God-power—and to the realization that this belief of two powers operates as a universal malpractice, an anti-Christ, a nothingness, then gradually do you become free. There are no material or mental powers that can operate in the consciousness of an individual who lives in the realization that God's grace is his sufficiency.

When you become free, you may well ask yourself, "Did God do something for me today that God was not doing before?" No, God was doing it all the time, only now you have removed the barrier from yourself. If there are clouds hiding the sun from you, in proportion as those clouds are dissolved, the sun will reveal itself as having been there all the time. Remember that there is no such thing as time, just as there are no degrees of evil. Then you will find that the good which comes into your experience today was there all the time, merely awaiting the removal of the barrier, and the barrier is the universal belief in a power of good and a power of evil which you have accepted.

Certainly, through the acceptance of two powers, mental and material laws do operate, and these laws are both good and evil. It is only when we no longer have powers of any kind that we no longer have good mental or material power and bad mental or material power.

REVEALING THE SPIRITUAL NATURE OF OUR BEING

We do not want to make the mistake of denying matter or mind. But let us understand that there is no good matter or bad matter, and there is no good mind or bad mind: there is only unconditioned mind [3] without qualities of good or evil because God is unconditioned Being. There cannot be a good God or an evil God; and therefore there cannot be good or evil in manifestation.

So it is with Spirit; Spirit is infinite and omnipresent, not good and not bad. Mind is not good or bad; it is just mind— unconditioned. When that truth becomes an integral part of our consciousness, we can look at this world and, instead of seeing a conditioned universe, we will begin to perceive it as it really is. When we can look at this universe without judgment as to what or who is good or evil, it will express back to us that which it is.

That is why, when we are with anyone who is ill, we close our eyes to the appearance and do not acknowledge him to be sick or well. Furthermore, he is not going to be any more spir-

[3] For a complete discussion of this subject, see the author's "Unconditioned Mind" in *The Thunder of Silence* (New York, N.Y.: Harper and Row, 1961).

itual when he is well than when he is sick. So changing him from being sick into being well is not spiritualizing him, nor is it beholding him as the Christ.

We are not interested in health as such: we are interested in the Christ of individual being, the spiritual nature of being, and that means beholding a person as neither good nor evil, but as spiritual, as the child of God. That means working with the sick, but not caring momentarily whether they are sick or well because we are busy bearing witness to the Christ of their being, that which knows neither good nor evil, that which is neither sick nor well, that which is neither young nor old. Healing work is only incidental to revealing the spiritual nature of our being which has in it qualities of neither good nor evil, qualities of neither youth nor age, qualities of neither life nor death.

Each one of us, as a spiritual being, is a manifestation of God, an actual expression of God-being. We have been given the full dominion of God, which we show forth in various ways by means of various talents or abilities. Each of these is a facet of God, and we can be full and complete, showing forth whatever our particular gift may be.

As human beings, we are not showing forth that fulfillment because we are limited by this same old belief of good and evil, youth and age, hereditary law and environment—all the limitations that have been placed upon us. But in the first realization that we have of the true nature of being, unconditioned and unfettered by beliefs of good and evil, we also find that we have become a more complete expression of God, a fuller expression of intelligence, love, joy, talent, ability, and capacity, and these grow as our own freedom increases.

TRANSITION AS UNFOLDING CONSCIOUSNESS

When we are on the spiritual path, we are laying up spiritual consciousness, and as we leave this plane, which eventually we do—not by death, but by transition—we find ourselves on an ascending scale, always going up, further into the light, further into freedom. There is really only one freedom in all this world: the freedom from the belief in good and evil. When we are free of that, we are truly free of physical, mental, moral, and financial limitations.

Fear comes in when we believe that some condition is going to lead to death. Nobody really fears pain of itself. It is only that pain may lead to death—that is what is feared. We may dislike pain, but we do not fear it, not until the thought of death accompanies it. But the thought of death could not frighten anyone who had ever experienced God, for he would know beyond all doubt that there is no power in death. "Yea, though I walk through the valley of the shadow of death, I will fear no evil," [4] for there are no powers: no destructive powers, no negative powers, no limiting powers.

To pass on, to die, to leave this world—however you want to express it—in a sense of freedom means to emerge into freedom with even less bondage to the belief in two powers and then to live in greater freedom in the transitional stage in which we find ourselves. Always remember the basic premise: God is eternal and immortal, and that means that you and I are eternal and immortal because there is no life but the life of God. That is why you will learn that there is no such thing as young life or old life. There is only life, and it is an immortal and eternal life from which we cannot escape by dying.

If you die while still in material sense, you can awaken only in that same material sense, a materiality which may be greatly

[4] Psalm 23:4.

intensified. The belief in limitation with which you leave this plane becomes greater limitation, but the degree of freedom with which you leave here becomes a greater freedom. The person who goes on from here in material sense, fearing and hating the experience, and squeezing himself into it, finds himself more tightly bound than before the transition; whereas the person leaving this plane in spiritual light is wide open for the experience, open to receive more light, more light, more light, and thereby finds himself less fettered on emerging from this plane into his new experience.

CONSCIOUSNESS IS ALWAYS EMBODIED

Many persons are puzzled about whether or not we take the body with us when we pass on. It must be understood first of all that consciousness always has form. Consciousness has to be embodied, and therefore we are never separated from body, from the form our consciousness assumes. It is true that our physical body is left for burial or cremation, but actually it is not our body that is left. It is our concept of what body is. We will never be without a body. Even if a person should rise so high as to learn how to travel through the air without an airplane, he would find that he is still embodied.

But actually, we are not now *in* a body. If a surgeon could examine us from the topmost hair of our heads to our toenails, he would never find us because we are not in the body. We are not in the body at all; we never were and we never can be. We exist separate and apart from our body, but we use the body as an instrument. In speaking of the body, the Master said, "Destroy this temple, and in three days I will raise it up." [5]

The day will come when it will be necessary for us to lay down this body because we will be ready for another experi-

[5] John 2:19.

ence, but in laying it down, it does not mean that we will be bodiless. It merely means that through our consciousness we will have built for ourselves another body.

It can be likened to the experience of those who have come to the United States from the ghettos of foreign countries. They come here, and some of them remain in ghettos, but as their consciousness grows, improves, and expands, they outgrow the ghettos in which they have lived, and eventually find themselves living in a far more wholesome environment. Their consciousness has built for them a better country to live in, a better neighborhood, and a better financial structure, and even though their relatives may still be living in a ghetto back in their homeland, the drive in the consciousness of some immigrants has built for them a more satisfactory home.

It is always individual consciousness that performs the miracles of life. If we are not satisfied with our present place in life, our consciousness will build a new one for us by enriching itself with spiritual truth. As consciousness is enriched, the body improves: the physical body, the mental body, the mind, the home, and the bank account. All these expand as consciousness is imbued with spiritual truth.

THE EVER-PRESENCE AND AVAILABILITY OF ILLUMINED CONSCIOUSNESS

The Soul or the life of an individual never dies, nor does it lose its attained development. Therefore, Jesus the Christ who left this experience in full illumination still exists and lives. He does not live in any place. He lives in and as consciousness, and since consciousness is infinite, he lives and exists in your consciousness and in mine, and it is within our power to receive light and instruction from that consciousness which forever has been, is now, and forever can be identified as Jesus Christ.

Gautama the Buddha who left this plane in full illumination

still lives, still teaches, and still performs his mighty works, and this is all being done in consciousness, and that means in your consciousness and my consciousness. We are being illumined and instructed by that state of consciousness. And so we could go on and on and find that all those who have attained illumination and who have left this plane fully illumined are right here where we are. They are here and are facing us through our own consciousness, and if we have not yet known that all spiritual light is embodied within our consciousness, we should become aware of it now.

The kingdom of God, of Allness, is within us, and we are being instructed of God. If, at this moment, it appears to be coming through a book, that is only a temporary situation, just as when it came through Jesus Christ at the time when he was physically present on earth. Jesus left this plane, but spiritual illumination continued because it remained in individual consciousness. And as your spiritual teacher passes from this experience, spiritual illumination will continue within you. Throughout all ages, spiritual teachers, revelators, and leaders will appear in the consciousness of man to speak the language of the day.

We have had need of every mental and spiritual teaching that has appeared on earth because each one has been a steppingstone to where we are today in The Infinite Way, which, through the principles it has revealed, is preparing consciousness for the day when no one will have to think in terms of a carnal mind because there will not even be the temptation of a carnal mind there.

That is the state of mysticism. That is when the individual no longer has to impersonalize because in a God-realized consciousness there is no evil to behold. That is the mystical state, and it is from that state of consciousness that the mystics and the mystical literature have come forth into experience.

In proportion as you learn to impersonalize, you are prepar-

ing yourself for that experience because you are training yourself for a state of mind in which evil has no reality, no power,
no law, no person, no cause. When you have come to that
place, you have that mind which was also in Christ Jesus, a
mind that can look at your particular Pilate and say, "Thou
hast no power"; that can look at the cripple and say, "What
did hinder you?"; that can look at the blind man and say,
"Open your eyes." In that state of consciousness, there are no
opposing powers.

Across the Desk

The spiritual life has a starting point which is common to all:
reconciliation. Naturally, since I and the Father are one, I must
first consciously reconcile myself to God by abiding in His
Spirit and His love. Practically, this means acknowledging
Spirit as the Cause, Substance, and Law unto myself and to all
that is, ascribing all power unto Spirit and no power to form
except that that form be all that invisible Spirit is. It means
acknowledging Omnipresence, Omniscience, Omnipotence as
the reality of my being, of my Self.

Hereby am I reconciled to God, but this is not sufficient.
Before I can go to the altar to pray, I must be reconciled to my
fellow man: friend and foe, near and far. "I and my Father are
one," [6] and therefore, reconciliation with my fellow man
means recognizing and acknowledging that God is the Self of
everyone. Now, in my conscious oneness with God, I am consciously one with my fellow man.

That is not yet enough. God is likewise the substance, intelligence, and law of all the universe: of the sun, moon, stars, and
planets; of the earth and all that therein is: the fish in the wa-

[6] John 10:30.

ters, the birds in the air, the crops beneath and above the ground, the gold and silver and gems. Verily, "the earth is the Lord's, and the fulness thereof." [7] In this realization, we are fully reconciled, and now I am one with God and one with the infinite forms as which It appears. This must even include weather and climate, and the laws of nature. In this reconciliation, my conscious oneness with God constitutes my oneness with all spiritual being and idea.

Please study the chapter "Conscious Oneness" in *The World Is New*.[8] When you read in the opening chapter of this book, "The world is new to every Soul when Christ has entered in," remember that the Christ enters every Soul at the moment of reconciliation to God and to every manifestation of Its being. The act of reconciliation is love in action.

Since the first step in reconciliation is the recognition of your Christ-Self, the second step must be the recognition of the Christ-Self of everyone. Would we now defile ourselves, knowing our true identity and the divine nature of our being? Could we possibly defile another, cheat, lie, defraud, debase anyone, anywhere, any time?

Watch the miracle of your rebirth through reconciliation. Observe how the laws of nature work *with* you, how even the weather and climate bless you. Observe that the animal and bird worlds become reconciled to you. This is a miracle of The Infinite Way of life.

[7] Psalm 24:1.
[8] By the author. (New York, N.Y.: Harper and Row, 1962).

10) "It Shall Not Come Nigh Thee"

If you have studied the preceding chapters carefully, you should be beginning to understand that the universal belief of good and evil operates hypnotically upon every person in the world. Every phase of discord that comes into any person's experience is a mesmeric influence from which he has not learned to protect himself. What with automobile collisions, sudden storms, and even coconuts falling from the trees, a person who leaves his home in the morning has no positive assurance that he will return safely at night.

Every morning of the week, safety engineers forecast approximately how many accidental deaths will occur that day. They cannot tell who will be the victims, but those casualties could be you or me or anyone else. Man has become a statistic. But no one wants to be a statistic. No one wants to fall victim to an accident.

How, then, can such mishaps and catastrophes be avoided?

Is there a way? Yes, there most certainly is, if those who have been taught the principles of one power, impersonalization, and "nothingization" can break through their mental inertia in the morning to the extent of consciously realizing:

> *There is but one Power operating in this universe. It is not a power of accident, death, disease, or sin. This Power is the same Power that causes the sun to rise and to set at its appointed time, and the tides to ebb and flow. The Power that is operating in this universe is the same Power that is operating in my consciousness, and It operates as the law unto my experience.*

> *There is no power in any mesmeric suggestion of accident. There is no power in any belief of infection or contagion. There is no power in the carnal mind, in any of its forms, or in any of its beliefs, individual or collective.*

"A thousand shall fall at thy side, and ten thousand at thy right hand; but it shall not come nigh thee."[1] To whom does that refer? To whom but the person who dwells "in the secret place of the most High"[2]—not one who dwells in a house, not one who dwells in an automobile or an airplane, but one who dwells "in the secret place of the most High."

YOUR EXPERIENCE IS YOUR STATE OF CONSCIOUSNESS OBJECTIFIED

Those are comforting words to read, but the all-important question before each and every person is: How can I arrive at that state of consciousness? How can I become the one who dwells "in the secret place of the most High"?

I can assure you that this is not brought about by sitting idly

[1] Psalm 91:7.
[2] Psalm 91:1.

by and accepting what the world doles out to you. It has to be done consciously. Whether you believe it or not, your life is either a conscious activity of your consciousness or the result of your unwillingness to let your consciousness express itself. You either become master of your fate and captain of your soul or you become a blotting paper for all the beliefs of good and evil that permeate the world, respond to them, and show them forth. You can become master of your fate only by an act of consciousness. This is not accomplished by the attitude, "Oh, God will take care of it." No, no, no! There must be an activity of truth in your consciousness, and that activity of truth has to be built stone upon stone.

No matter what form of meditation you practice, it has to be built around the principle that there is only one power, that nothing but God, and the activity of God, is power, and that any sense of evil is impersonal, the activity of the fleshly mind. Where you are makes no difference: whether you go up in an airplane or down in a submarine, or whether you are a soldier on a battle front or a farmer tilling his soil. Whatever the nature of the human picture, it has to be consciously met. Every treatment or meditation must embody these two principles: the realized truth that God Itself is infinite and the only power, and that every appearance is but a mesmeric influence, the temptation of the one impersonal evil coming to your consciousness to be accepted or rejected.

Remember that temptation, whatever its form, has to be consciously rejected. This is not easy to do because the one thing the world is suffering from is mental inertia. It will not wake up and think. It wants to look at pictures. It does not want to give voice to specific truth. It does not want to live with truth. It wants to depend on an unknown God, or on a concept of God that has failed mankind for thousands of years.

It is so easy to sit back and prate, "God will do it." But God will not do anything that He is not doing—and do not ever believe that God is going to do anything a minute from now that He is not doing now. Do not believe that you are ever going to know enough truth to influence God to do something for you or for anyone else. Do not think that you will ever be so spiritual that God is going to be your servant and fulfill your wishes, your hopes, or your desires. There is no such God.

God is. And God is "is-ing" this very second. God is being this very second, and God is being all that God can be. There is no way for God to change. God is the same yesterday, today, and forevermore. God is from everlasting to everlasting. Do not try to get God to be anything or do anything. God *is*.

The responsibility is on your shoulders. "Awake thou that sleepest, . . . and Christ shall give thee light." [3] Wake up to the fact that your experience is going to be your own state of consciousness objectified. If you persist in walking around all day without living consciously in the realization of God—omnipresent, omnipotent, and omniscient God here and now, the all and only Power—and without impersonalizing all phases of evil and realizing that they exist only as the "arm of flesh" [4] or nothingness, you will not bring harmony into your experience.

From the moment of waking in the morning to going to sleep at night, you should be doing protective work. But do not think of protective work in the sense of protecting yourself or anybody else from evil. Protective work is the realization that there is no power from which to protect yourself. It is living in the realization that since there is only one Power there are no powers to do anything or be anything, and any suggestion of some other power is a mesmeric influence. That is protective work.

Without this realization, even though you are not consciously thinking of accidents or discords, diseases, sins, or temptations, you are permitting yourself to accept uncon-

[3] Ephesians 5:14.
[4] II Chronicles 32:8.

sciously or subconsciously the world's mesmeric and hypnotic suggestions.

Error touches your life in much the same way as subliminal perception operates. Things enter your consciousness which you cannot see, hear, taste, touch, or smell. It is not necessary to see a headline to know that there is trouble in the world, because even though that trouble may not consciously be brought to your attention, you inwardly feel it.

You may awaken with a headache, with a dullness, or a sense of fear. None of this originates in you; none of this is a part of you. You may not have heard that there is an epidemic of flu, and yet the first thing you know is that you have come down with an attack of the flu. You were not exposed to it; you did not consciously entertain the idea of it, but that suggestion entered your consciousness. When there is not an inner protection, that is, the understanding that this hypnotic or mesmeric influence, this mental malpractice, or whatever you want to call it, is not power and is not an emanation of God, it can take root in you and appear in any and every form. That is why there are these human experiences of discord and inharmony.

WEATHER AS AN ACTIVITY OF MIND

Miracles will appear in your life when you practice these principles of spiritual living and when you can rise above living in this truth merely for your own sake or your family's, and begin to apply them to whatever touches your immediate world or the world at large—from government even to the weather.

Yes, even weather responds to a realization of spiritual principles. If that seems strange to you, think for a moment: Is weather something that is external to you? Is weather something that just happens? No, weather is an activity of mind, and because there is only one mind, weather is perfect. The only reason that we experience imperfect weather is because there is a belief in two powers which makes for good weather and bad weather.

I do not mean by this that you should get the idea that all days should be filled with sunshine, and that that would be an evidence of spiritual fruitage. What I mean is that no weather need be what we call bad, destructive, or of a nature that takes life or produces injuries. This must be demonstrated by students where situations involving destructive weather arise before we arrive at the point of proving it on a broader scale. Some of us have done that and have proved that destructive and injurious forms of weather can be dissolved through the understanding that weather exists as an activity of mind. If you do not believe this, try to think of weather without a mind to know that there is such a thing as weather.

There cannot be an activity outside mind. Which mind? You have no choice. There is only one mind, the instrument of that Consciousness which is the source of all action, all law, and all cause. When you behold anything unlike the activity of a spiritual law or life, it is only because of the acceptance of this belief in two powers, two laws, two minds.

Nothing happens ouside the activity of mind—not a thing. If it did, there would be nobody aware of it. If it is the activity of the mind of God, you cannot change it, you cannot alter it, you cannot improve it, and it would be quite futile to attempt to do so. Do not try to interfere with the movement of the stars, the sun, the moon, or the tides. These are activities of the divine Consciousness, the infinite, immortal Eternal, That which was before there was a human being to know it. But on the other hand, anything that exists as an activity of the carnal mind can be nullified in proportion to the degree of your awareness of these principles.

Watch this as it is related to weather. Watch it with tidal waves or with storms, and see how quickly they are dissipated when someone knows and understands that they are not conditions of matter: they are activities of the mesmeric mind. Watch how very often they stop instantaneously because they cannot last long in the face of that realization.

If you are threatened with a tidal wave or a hurricane and wish to avoid the experience, know this truth:

> *This threatening storm is not a thing—not a thing at all. It is an activity of the carnal mind, and the carnal mind has no law, being, substance, or cause. Therefore, this storm is nothing but an image in thought, and an image in thought has no power.*

Some years ago a citizen of a community asked for spiritual help for his city. It had rained steadily for eighteen months in that area, and many of the businessmen in the community were either bankrupt or on the verge of bankruptcy. After the help was given, there was no more rain, although the weather bureau reported that the rain would resume at any moment because the atmospheric conditions that had caused the uninterrupted rainfall were still present. But it did not rain! Then three days later the condition that was supposed to have caused the rain disappeared—but only three days after the rain had stopped! God does not stop rain: God knows nothing about rain.

Once you begin to realize that error—evil in any form—is merely the product of the universal mesmeric mind, and then "nothingize" it in the realization that it is not of God, it will make no difference to you whether it is weather, false appetite, sin, disease, lack, limitation, or unemployment. They will all disappear. They begin to disappear the moment you realize that they exist only as an activity of this universal mesmeric mind. But this mind is not God-ordained, and it has no God-law to support it. Your knowing that begins to dissolve the picture because all that it ever was, was a picture, an image in thought.

> *God made all that was made. God is the activity of the sun, the moon, the stars, and the planets. If it were not for the activity of God, there would be no crops in the ground, no oil, iron, or steel, no fish in the sea, and no birds in the air. All these things testify to the fact that the activity of God is infinite and omnipresent, always active.*

> *But I have just been told about an approaching storm. Yes, but what is it? Another form of mesmeric suggestion! Another activity of the carnal mind that would claim to operate as a condition! It is only a mental image in thought, without life, without law, without being.*

You build a consciousness of this truth by working with it. You may wake up in the morning and find some rather frightening weather outside. Then the very first thought that should come to you is, "Yes, but is it power?" If it is not power, what difference does it make if the newspapers call it good weather or bad weather? It is just weather. Who thus labels it as good or bad? The farmer who needs rain does not call rain bad. And the umbrella manufacturer does not think of rain as bad. The human being, Adam, calls things good and evil and gives them their names.

SAFETY AS AN ACTIVITY OF CONSCIOUSNESS

Once you know that anything that is the emanation of the carnal mind is without law, without God-being, God-presence, or God-power, you have begun to nullify it. If it does not yield the first time, keep at it a hundred times if necessary. Sometimes it takes hundreds of times of knowing the truth to break a situation. Undoubtedly, the Master at his height could have broken through any hypnotism immediately, but you and I are not at that level at present.

It is only the degree and the depth of your awareness that really meet a situation. So if you have not had a sufficient awareness today to meet an apparently unyielding situation, go back to a realization of the principles a second, third, or fourth time, and keep at it until the problem dissolves. The time will come when you will find that there will be very little human effort involved, very little mental effort, but that will come only as these principles are embodied within you and become real to you.

In the early stages of working consciously with these principles, whenever you receive suggestions of bad weather, accidents, sickness, sin, war, depressions, lack, or unemployment— as soon as these things touch your consciousness—it is necessary to be alert enough to know that this is the tempter. This is the temptation; this is a suggestion of a power and a presence apart from God. Then you must reject it in the realization that it is nothing but the fleshly mind. With that, you dismiss it, and that is the end of it. It takes only a minute, but in that minute you have consciously recognized within yourself the power of Truth, and Truth being infinite, nothing else can enter.

On every side, you are witnessing sin, disease, death, lack, limitation, unemployment, disfigurement, alcoholism, drug addiction, poverty. All these things confront you on the streets, in the press, and on the radio, and you cannot afford to be a blotting paper. You cannot afford to let those things enter your consciousness and take root. You must be consciously alert to realize, "Yes, these are pictures of sense; these are mental im-

ages—suggestions being presented to me—but in my understanding of one God, one power, one law, they are nothing."

Then you will find that you are abiding "in the secret place
of the most High," and none of these things will come nigh
your dwelling place—if not literally "none of these things," certainly few. And when they do come, you have a principle with
which to work to free yourself from the belief in them.

As far as I know, there are no human beings on earth who
have completely avoided all discords and inharmony—not even
those who have locked themselves away in monasteries or con-
vents—because that same old human mind follows them wherever they go, and it accepts these suggestions even when they
are not aware of them. There is no place where we can go to
hide from the world's troubles because wherever we go we
carry our mind with us, and if it is a receiving station for the
suggestions of the world, we do not have to see, hear, taste,
touch, or smell them in order to become aware of them. They
are in the atmosphere. Jesus referred to them as appearances
when he said, "Judge not according to the appearance, but
judge righteous judgment." [5] Everything that came to his
awareness was an appearance, and he never judged by what he
saw. He let it pass by in the realization that it was only an
appearance and could have no power.

LAYING UP SPIRITUAL TREASURES

As we engage in this practice, we will save ourselves from
many of the woes and negative experiences of this world, but
what is even more important is that once we have proved these
principles in our own experience, we will see how quickly our
conscious awareness of them begins to set others free. They do
not have to know that we are knowing the truth of their spirit-

[5] John 7:24.

ual identity, and yet many will receive healings without knowing the direction from which their help comes.

Since we are not seeking personal glory but only to witness a principle in operation, we need not be concerned about getting credit for any healing for which we may be the instrument. To us, the joy and the satisfaction are that we have discovered a principle of life that we can live by and which will benefit those who are receptive and responsive to it. Getting credit is a lot of nonsense, because it makes no difference how many medals are pinned on us while we are here or how many honors or titles we receive in this life, we cannot take them with us. Our money, stocks, and bonds we check at the probate court as we go out, and the medals, the titles, and the honors are taken down from the wall, stored away for a few years, and then burned. These are of no avail to us—not one bit. Even the good that is sometimes spoken of us is relatively unimportant because there are probably just as many saying the opposite about us.

What we do take with us as we leave this plane is every bit of good that we have brought into active expression in our life and every bit of spiritual enlightenment we have gained. These are stored up where neither "moth [nor] rust doth corrupt," [6] and these we take with us to become the foundation of our next experience. Every spiritual principle of life that we embody becomes our state of consciousness thoughout all time, just as every skill that we attain here is ours throughout our experience here. The spiritual principles we learn are our protection, our health, safety, security, and peace; and we know that as the world awakens to this truth, these are the principles that will eventually bring about freedom for every individual on the face of the globe.

At first, it is hard work to apply these principles throughout

[6] Matthew 6:19.

the day because we forget more often than we remember. It is usually ten or eleven o'clock in the morning before we remember how much we have forgotten that we should have been consciously knowing since seven o'clock, and then we have to start in at noon to make up for lost time. By the time we get into bed at night, we have really gotten ourselves into a jam because then we have to get up to undo all the forgetting we have done throughout the day. It is a strict discipline for at least a year, and oftentimes much longer than that.

You will understand what I mean if you try just such a simple thing as making an agreement with yourself that you will never eat a bite of food of any kind or drink a drop of any kind of liquid without consciously recognizing that God is the source. Then at the end of the day count how many times you have forgotten this, and you will know how difficult it is.

But, on the other hand, watch the magical effects in your life when you do reach that place where you consciously recognize with every bite of food that but for God it would not be there for you to consume, that but for God's grace you would not have it because it would not be on earth, and but for God's grace you would not be able to digest it.

Come to the realization that the most trifling acts of your day, such as waking up in the morning or sleeping at night, cannot be performed without an activity of this invisible Spirit, and observe what happens when you begin to acknowledge Him in all your ways. Notice what happens as you consciously remember when you get into your automobile that God drives not only your car but, since there is only one Being, one Selfhood, God is the driver behind the wheel of every car. Your conscious recognition of this sets you free from statistical beliefs.

For a long, long time, this is hard work. This is not an easy path, but eventually something beautiful begins to happen.

You no longer have to think consciously. Thoughts come of their own accord, automatically arising within you, and you really understand what Paul meant when he said, "I live; yet not I, but Christ liveth in me." [7] After that there is very little of conscious effort. It all flows from within.

[7] Galatians 2:20.

11) Lifting Up the I

There is no one mode, means, method, or system which can correctly be called metaphysical or spiritual healing. In fact, there are as many different approaches to spiritual healing as there are in *materia medica* with its allopathy, homeopathy, osteopathy, chiropractic, and naprapathy, all different forms of *materia medica*.

In the world of metaphysical and spiritual healing, there are the evangelists who, by the grace of God, have received some special state of consciousness through which they heal without knowing how, why, or wherefore. For the most part, they do not have the slightest idea of any principle involved in healing: they only know that healings do take place, sometimes through the spoken word and sometimes through the laying on of hands. Apparently, it is something that is just a part of their being, something that has come to them at a particular period in their life, and something over which they have no control.

Then there are those approaches to healing which employ mental means and, by suggestion, attempt to change a diseased or evil condition into a good one. There are also methods which attempt to combine the mental and the spiritual.

A person who has had any experience with other forms of metaphysical or spiritual healing and decides to practice healing through Infinite Way healing principles may have to unlearn most of what he has previously known in order to grasp these principles, and if he encounters difficulty on the way it is probably because he has not yet unlearned enough.

AN UNDERSTANDING OF IMMORTALITY, BASIC TO HEALING

The Infinite Way begins with an infinite, ever present, omnipotent God. Its premise is that there is no imperfection in any part of God or of God's creation, none whatsoever! God is perfect being, and so, therefore, is God's creation. No one was ever born, and no one will ever die; no one ever had a beginning, and no one will ever have an ending.

One way to understand the continuity of life is through the word "I." This *I*, which is our identity, is actually coexistent with God. It is the eternal part of our being. It has no knowledge of birth or death. It is that part of our being which has existed for billions of years, and will continue to exist without interruption for many more billions of years. As long as there is God, there will be a "you" and a "me" because we are one with God: "I and my Father are one," [1] and not two. The *I* which I am and the *I* which is God are one and the same *I*, and therefore, *I* is immortal.

Very often, when we think of immortality, we think of life beyond the grave, but we do not stop to realize that if there is

1 John 10:30.

any truth to immortality it must also mean life before birth. We cannot be immortal if we have a life that ever began: immortality is from everlasting to everlasting. God can no more begin than He can end, and if God and I are one, the *I* of me, in that oneness, has never begun and will never end.

Our identity remains intact, spiritual, and perfect, not only after the grave, but it was so even before we were born. Our life from the cradle to the grave is that experience which has been likened to a parenthesis, but when the parenthesis is removed we live in the full circle of immortality. It is true that while we may be aware of ourselves as living only in this particular parenthesis, slowly or rapidly moving from birth to death, actually it is possible for this parenthesis to be removed and for us to become aware of our true identity as one with the entire circle of life and its immortality and eternality.

Once we can realize ourselves as *I,* separate and apart from personality, separate and apart from a physical body, as *I,* the incorporeal, spiritual *I,* we will have the secret of the eternality and immortality of life: without beginning, without birth; without ending, without death.

Since the *I* that God is and the *I* that we are, are one, we can understand that the infinite perfection of God is the infinite perfection of our being. "Son, thou art ever with me, and all that I have is thine." [2] This does not refer to material things: dollar bills, bank accounts, property, fur coats, or automobiles. "All that *I* have" means all the immortality, spirituality, integrity, all the life, all the perfection, all the holiness of God. All that is of God is of you and of me because the *I* of you and of me and the *I* of God are one and the same *I,* and all the qualities of God are the qualities of spiritual, eternal, immortal man: of you and of me.

This is the premise in Infinite Way healing work, and if we

[2] Luke 15:31.

want to heal, we must first of all remind ourselves of this truth. We must be conscious of the truth that the *I* of you and of me and the *I* of God are one, and all that constitutes the *I* of God constitutes the *I* of you and of me, for we are forever one with the Father. All that is of God is ours: all the immortality, eternality, spiritual perfection, harmony, peace, justice, infinity.

DISCORD, THE FRUITAGE OF SOWING TO THE FLESH

When we have established ourselves in that spiritual truth, the next question on which we must be clear is: But what about this sin, this disease, this false appetite, this lack or limitation, this unemployment, this lost baggage?

All the writings of The Infinite Way clearly reveal where evil comes from and why it comes. They explain its relation to karmic law, as it is called in the Orient, or the as-ye-sow-so-shall-ye-reap of the Bible. "He that soweth to his flesh shall of the flesh reap corruption; but he that soweth to the Spirit shall of the Spirit reap life everlasting." [3] And the Master taught, "He that abideth in me, and I in him, the same bringeth forth much fruit." [4] If we do not abide in the Word and let the Word abide in us, we will be as a branch of a tree that is cut off, withers, and dies. Every moment of every day determines what our tomorrows will be. As we sow, in this moment, so will we reap tomorrow, next week, next year, or ten years from now.

This teaching has often been interpreted to mean that if we obey the Ten Commandments we are sowing good and will reap good; and if we disobey the Ten Commandments, we are sowing to the flesh and will reap corruption. This is utter non-

[3] Galatians 6:8.
[4] John 15:5.

sense. It has no such meaning whatsoever! The as-ye-sow-so-shall-ye-reap doctrine means that if we abide in the spiritual truth of being, we will reap harmony because then we are sowing to the Spirit and will reap spiritual fruitage. But if we accept the world's belief in two powers, its belief in Spirit and matter, in good and evil, then we are going to experience both good and evil.

While we are part of this human race into which we were born, we are sowing to the flesh, and we are going to reap corruption, even if we obey the Ten Commandments to the letter. This is what the Master meant when he said to his followers, "Except your righteousness shall exceed the righteousness of the scribes and Pharisees, ye shall in no case enter into the kingdom of heaven." [5] These two Hebrew sects lived in complete obedience to the laws of the Temple. They dotted every "i" and crossed every "t." They spent every moment required by theological law in worship; they observed every feast day, every fast day, and every holiday; they tithed; they sacrificed; they lived up to the Ten Commandments and to all the laws of the Temple, but Jesus said, "Your righteousness [must] exceed" that of those persons who are 100 per cent perfect! It sounds impossible, but it is not.

If we sow to the Spirit, we will be obeying the Ten Commandments without even being aware of so doing and without any temptation to do otherwise. Therefore, we do not have to concern ourselves with the Ten Commandments. What we have to concern ourselves with is to abide in the spiritual word of truth. This is not easy of accomplishment because it means that what we accept into our consciousness is going to determine our experience. We have to begin with the acceptance of the universal belief in good and evil, and we have to reject that and say to ourselves, "No, I accept neither good nor evil: I

[5] Matthew 5:20.

accept only God, Spirit, as infinite All, and in God there is neither good nor evil: there is only spiritual, perfect, harmonious being."

When Satan stands in front of us insisting that there are two powers—spiritual powers and material or mental powers—we have to be quiet enough so that the *I* of us can reply, "No, no, I accept God; I accept spiritual being as the All. I accept the scriptural truth that nothing can enter God 'that defileth . . . or maketh a lie,'⁶ nothing! Only God is God, and God is infinite perfection, so there cannot be powers of good and of evil; there cannot be spiritual powers and mental or material powers. There can be only God-power, infinite, spiritual God-power." This refusal to accept in our consciousness good and evil, spiritual and material or mental powers, and this holding steadfastly to the word *I* is sowing to the Spirit.

CONCESSIONS IMPOSED BECAUSE OF LIVING IN
"THIS WORLD"

We are constantly faced with good persons and bad persons, but we cannot accept either good persons or bad persons, sick persons or well persons: we must accept only the children of God, spiritual identity.

It is true that in our daily affairs and in our speech we make concessions to appearances. For example, every time anyone asks a practitioner for help, and he responds with "I will give you help," that is a concession to appearances, but it is something that must be done. No one can be completely absolute in such a situation and say, "No, I will not give you any help because you are already perfect."

The patient's response would very likely be, "Well, if you won't give me any help, then I will find somebody who will."

⁶ Revelation 21:27.

So an Infinite Way practitioner makes concessions and says, "Of course, I will give you help at once," but within himself, he cannot believe that. The *I* of him has to be knowing inwardly, "No, the *I* which is God is my Self, and the *I* which is God is your Self. There is only one Power; there is only one Presence; there is only one Law; there is only one Being." By the time the practitioner has attained this realization, the patient will probably be beginning to feel better. Nevertheless a concession to the call for help has been made, and in a measure we do that in all our affairs.

Politically, we will speak of one candidate as a good candidate, and another as a bad one. This is only a part of the human drama. Inwardly, we realize that for voting purposes we are judging those candidates from a personal standpoint in terms of our own frame of reference. Actually, we know better: we know that *I* am he. Even though he does not know it, we know! If we are not knowing that the *I* of me is the *I* of you, and the *I* of you and of me is the *I* of God, for we are one, we are sowing to the flesh.

So it is that in normal, everyday conversation, especially with those who are not on this Path, in speaking of the weather, the climate, germs, and all other so-called material powers, we are not going to argue with anyone and try to show how bright we are, or how stupid. "Agree with thine adversary." [7] Do not start an argument with anyone who is talking about what bad weather, bad crops, or bad times we are having. It is not so important what we do in the way of lip service: what counts is what we are doing within.

[7] Matthew 5:25.

SEEING THROUGH UNIVERSAL BELIEFS IN THE
AREA OF RELATIONSHIPS

In no area is this better illustrated than with parents and their children. There are many occasions when parents have to discipline their children, and times when they may appear quite angry with them; but they must be sure that they are doing this only outwardly, not inwardly. In their hearts, they cannot accept this. Their outward show of displeasure is only for the purpose of correcting the young, immature thought that could not possibly grasp this idea of perfection in one explanation and, because of the universal belief, could not live up to it.

For the most part, children are not children at all: they are just ages. There are one-year-olds, two-year-olds, six-year-olds, and twelve-year-olds. Those falling into a particular age bracket act alike, and they are very much alike in their responses. It is only through the spiritual work and training of their parents that eventually they become individuals, but left to themselves, they all pattern their conduct according to the accepted standard of their peers at the different ages through which they pass. But this can be changed as parents understand that what they are being faced with as ugly behavior on the part of their child is merely a belief, universal to that age group.

In the same way, we can bring out a different relationship with our neighbor and with the persons that we deal with in business, not so much by acting differently outwardly as by an inward realization of the truth of their identity. They are neither good nor bad; they are neither sick nor well; they are neither rich nor poor: they are spiritual. Spirit has no shifting, changing qualities, and Its only quantity is infinity. To sow to the Spirit we must be continuously entertaining a spiritual awareness, having uppermost in our consciousness a spiritual understanding of the nature of God, man, and the universe. We must inwardly know that the only law is spiritual law, and in the knowing of this, mental and material laws are nullified.

Once we have raised up the *I* in ourselves, so that this *I* that does not accept appearances is governing our experience, we will less and less accept powers of good and evil, or material and mental powers, but will recognize only spiritual power. This *I* that we have raised up within us that will not permit a negative thought to get past It, this *I* now governs our life and the lives of those who turn to us.

This *I* we have had with us from the beginning. We brought It into this world with us, but because of the world's ignorance of truth, we also came into the world ignorant of truth. Because of that ignorance, what handled us, therefore, what has governed our lives, and what now governs the lives of all human beings is a form of hypnotism or malpractice—whatever it is that makes us think good and evil, hear good and evil, see good and evil, and act from the standpoint of good and evil. In short, it is whatever makes us accept appearances at face value.

"JUDGE RIGHTEOUS JUDGMENT"

Those who are not familiar with the optical illusions engendered by atmospheric conditions on the desert will probably accept the appearance of a big beautiful lake with a wonderful city built around it which looms up before them, and will start driving their car toward that beautiful lake, even looking for a hotel where they can spend the night. However, those who understand the phenomenon of a mirage do not for a moment accept the appearance of a lake or a city at face value: they instantly recognize that this is mirage.

In "this world," where an ignorance of truth predominates, we are constantly being faced with sin, disease, death, lack, and limitation, with evil of every kind. We accept the world of appearances and pay the penalty for that acceptance. If, on the other hand, we have been spiritually taught, we will instantly recognize that these suggestions that come to us are appearances like the mirage on the desert. The Master taught, "Judge not according to the appearance, but judge righteous judgment." [8] So I say to you, "Having eyes, do you not see through this appearance? Having ears, do you not hear beyond this appearance? Do not accept appearances of good and evil at face value. Accept them only as mirage, illusion, a form of malpractice, or hypnotism, and above all things, do not accept them as something that has to be healed, reformed, changed, or corrected."

Every day we meet up with material laws, mental laws, and legal laws. Every day we meet up with appearances of sin, false appetite, disease, evil men in government, and spiritual wickedness in high places. There is not a day in which these suggestions do not cross our path. We cannot avoid them, not by going away to a convent, a monastery, or an ashrama because wherever we are we take the world right with us. Wherever we go, the newspapers will shout, and the radios will blare.

As a matter of fact, the higher we go in spiritual realization, the more of evil and discordant appearances will be brought to our doorstep, because sick persons, sinning persons, and poor persons gravitate to those of spiritual light to pour out their burdens. And this is right; it is right! The Christ of us says, "Drop your burdens at My feet. My yoke is light. Just pour them all out. They are of no weight to Me."

We really do not have to get rid of any of the sins, diseases, lacks, or limitations of the persons who come to us. We merely have to refuse to accept the appearances and realize that whatever is presented to us is a state of hypnotism producing an illusion, a mirage.

[8] John 7:24.

We must stand fast in spite of every appearance, in spite of every cry of pain, in spite of everything: *I* within you and *I* within me must stand fast and not accept it. Because the *I* within us has been lifted up, we see through the mirage to Reality. In God's kingdom, there is not a sin, disease, death, lack, or limitation. In the whole of God's kingdom, there is not an evil of any nature. We have to stand fast in that truth, and let the appearances hit up against us until they break.

Some of them break rapidly, some of them will not break so rapidly, and a few refuse to break at all. Why? One reason may be that as practitioners we are not rising quite as high into heavenly consciousness as we should be. I will admit that if our practitioners could be a little more separate and apart from the ways of the world they could do better works, but because we all have to live in this world and with it, it may be that we do not rise high enough in spiritual consciousness to do all the works that we should do.

The other reason is that the patients will not yield. They usually have in mind the changing of an evil condition into a good one, and this acts as a block. Spiritual healing is not changing an evil condition into a good one: healing is really the changing of consciousness, and very often there is a reluctance or unwillingness to yield up whatever it is that is acting as a block.

This is never done consciously. We never blame anyone for whatever it is that he is holding onto because he cannot help it, any more than we can help whatever it is that we hold onto. It is something deep down in our consciousness, and the answer lies in keeping on until there is a yielding.

WE CANNOT GET RID OF AN APPEARANCE

In Infinite Way healing work, we are not turning to God to heal anybody. We do not have the kind of God who would let anyone be sick if it were within His knowledge, and if we recognize God to be Omniscience and Omnipotence we surely could not find anyone outside of God's knowledge. It is entirely a matter of the individual called a practitioner being able to rise to that state of consciousness which refuses to accept the appearance, knowing its hypnotic and illusory source, and the nothingness of it because it is not supported by a law of God.

No sin and no disease are supported by a law of God. If they were, they would be eternal. We can never hope to change anything that is supported by God. If it has a law of God to maintain it, we cannot hope to break it, and the very fact that we do break through our sins, our diseases, and our lacks is sufficient proof that there never was any law of God supporting them. A law of matter, yes; a law of mind, yes; but these are not laws of God, and for this very reason, any form of evil can be dispelled.

We need never be afraid to try to heal, regardless of the name or nature of the claim, because, to begin with, we have the awareness that there is no law of God supporting or maintaining any erroneous condition; and we know that no law of God created it. God never made it.

Humanly it is true that we are sick and we die; but let us this moment free ourselves from the superstition that God has anything to do with any of this, and let us put the blame on our own shoulders. It is our ignorance, yours and mine, nobody else's; but if it is your ignorance and mine, it is only our ignorance because we are a part of the universal ignorance which has been handed down to us.

Anyone can undertake healing work at any time if he will realize the basic principle that he is not trying to remove a disease, a condition, a sin, or a false appetite. The moment anyone tries to do that, he is trapped, and there will be no healing.

We are not dealing with a sin, with a disease, with a false appetite, or with a lack. We are dealing with an illusory appearance that must be recognized as having no God-law, God-ordination, God-presence, or God-power. We are not dealing with a condition, but with a universal belief in a selfhood apart from God. Any condition or situation is always a universal belief, always a universal claim. It is never the fault of our patient; it is never the fault of our student; it is never the fault of ourselves: it is a universal claim of two powers, a universal claim of a selfhood apart from God, a universal belief in good and evil. But the truth is *I*:

> *I and the Father are one. All that is true of the Father is true of me because of oneness. God is Spirit, and I am spiritual. God is immortal and eternal, and I am immortal and eternal.*

This is not only the truth about us: it is the truth about the patient, the student, or anyone who has called upon us for help.

We are dealing with an appearance, an appearance produced by a universal malpractice, a universal ignorance, a universal hypnotism, *but only an appearance.* We are not to attempt to get rid of the appearance. *We can no more get rid of an appearance than we can get rid of the mirage on the desert.* We can only see through it and understand it to be a mirage, and then go on about our business. Usually in the moment of our recognizing it as mirage, the picture dissolves. So it is, too, in healing. In our realization of the illusory nature of the appearance, the appearance dissolves, and then the patient says, "I am better," or "I am healed."

DO'S AND DON'T'S IN HEALING WORK

In The Infinite Way, we never give a treatment to a person. We give the treatment to ourselves. We are the one under treatment because we are the one to whom the appearance has been brought, and it must be met in our own consciousness. We never touch the mind of our patient or student: we never enter his mental home. We have no business there! Every person is a sacred being, sacred unto God, and we do not intrude into his mind or thought. If we do, we are practicing hypnotism or suggestion, and we are meddling in somebody else's mind. That is no part of The Infinite Way. In fact, we never mention a patient's name in our treatment; we never mention the name of his disease, sin, or fear, nor do we ever reach out to send a thought to him. Never! To do so is a serious offense in a spiritual teaching!

What we do when the appearance is brought to us is to go immediately to the *I* of our being, and abide there until we come to the conclusion that "I and my Father are one," and that this is a universal truth. We wrestle with this truth within ourselves until we come to the point of conviction that there is only Spirit. This teaching does not permit anyone ever, under any circumstance, to enter the mind or thought of a patient or to address him by name and say, "You are well," or "You are spiritual." None of that is acceptable practice in The Infinite Way!

When in The Infinite Way a person says, "I have a headache," I immediately forget him and deal with myself. The appearance of a headache has been presented to me; the appearance of a sick person has been presented to me. What am I going to do with it? And so I realize, "Ah, Joel, you are not going to accept that for one single moment. You know better! You know that 'I and my Father are one,' and that you have nothing to do with healing any person out there! You know, Joel, that all that God is, you are. You know that there is only spiritual law, spiritual being. You know that there are not good people and bad people; you know that there are not sick people and well people. You are dealing with God and His perfect spiritual creation, and all other appearances are but the product of a universal hypnotism, a universal malpractice, a universal belief in two powers."

If I keep that up within myself, eventually it comes, "Ah, yes, that is truth." Then I am quiet, and in a few moments a deep sense of peace comes, a "click," a deep breath, something or other, and I know that God is on the scene, and that is all there is to it. As you can see, I have had nothing to do with the patient.

The person may call, write, or cable me an hour later or the next day, and I may have to go through this same process again. If he does not respond quickly, I may have to stay with him for months and months, but the procedure is always the same. Never do I work through suggestion; never do I work through hypnotism; never will I enter the consciousness of any person.

My object is not merely to change a person's sickness into health. My object is to lift him in consciousness, not by doing something to him, but by raising up the *I* in me, and then, if *I* be lifted up, he is drawn to that level of consciousness, but without my having to do anything humanly about it, or about him as a person.

That is why it is necessary, first, to establish ourselves in the absolute conviction that there is a "My kingdom," ⁹ a spiritual kingdom, and that nothing "that defileth . . . or maketh a lie" ¹⁰ can ever enter that spiritual kingdom of God and His spiritual universe and spiritual man.

PRACTICE IS ESSENTIAL

Through conscious realization we must establish the truth of our oneness with God, our oneness with spiritual perfection. Then, from there on, we are not dealing with persons or condi-

9 John 18:36.
10 Revelation 21:27.

tions: we are dealing only with the world of appearances, or illusion. The illusion in one place may be a lake, and the illusion in another may be a city, but it is all illusion, and the substance of an illusion is nothingness, whether it appears as a lake or a city. The substance of illusion is the same, whether it appears as a cold, a headache, a cancer, tuberculosis, a broken bone, poverty, or unemployment. It is always nothingness, the "arm of flesh," [11] appearance. Behind it is the activity of a universal malpractice or hypnotism, which is produced by the universal belief in two powers.

The healing principle of The Infinite Way is simple, but no one can bring about healings quickly just through knowing the letter of truth: it is working with it that develops this consciousness. It becomes second nature not to take in the appearance as if it were a condition, not to condemn a person, not to react to any appearance presented by a person, and that is when the healing consciousness is in full bloom, and then is when our healing ministry begins. Up to that time, we are practicing, practicing, and practicing to develop that consciousness. The consciousness that does not respond to appearances, the consciousness that is aware of the spiritual nature of creation and of the illusory nature of appearances, is a healing consciousness.

Every serious student must work with these principles and practice them with the most insignificant claims that arise. Many times letters come hesitatingly asking for help for a cat or a dog. My answer always is the same: "I am not interested in whether it is your cat or your dog: I am interested in the appearance that is being presented to me, and that is what must be met." By meeting it when it appears in their cats or their dogs, later on they are enabled to see how to meet it in a human being. Never, never for a moment think that there is

[11] II Chronicles 32:8.

anything so small, so tiny, or so insignificant that these principles should not be applied to it, because I can assure you that in
applying them to the small things of life, you help to develop
the consciousness for undertaking the greater ones.

Keep yourself in the consciousness into which this lesson lifts
you because it is all too easy to come down to the human level
and be frightened by an appearance of disease, sin, or lack,
whether that appearance is presented as a child or a grown-up.
It is only by abiding in these principles that fear is dissipated,
and automatically every error is wiped out through the recognition: illusion, hypnotism, malpractice, an appearance! The
more you can deal with all error in that way, the better healing
work you will accomplish.

The deeper you go into the healing consciousness, the more
you find yourself living so in meditation that you do not have
to go into a deep meditation with every claim that comes because you are in it nine tenths of the time. You will find, however, that it is necessary to go into meditation ten, twenty, or
thirty times a day, not for the sake of meeting a specific call,
but in order to maintain that inner communion constantly.
Then the calls can come thick and fast, and no specific meditation is necessary because you are living in that *I* which has
been lifted up in you, the *I* which is the healer.

But I warn you: if your patients are not getting the results
that they should get, it is because you are not meditating often
or deeply enough to bring forth that depth of realization of
God that is necessary. There is no such thing in this work as
merely saying piously, "Oh, let God do it." There is no God on
the field until you have brought God on to the field by this
inner realization.

Do not forget that there would be no sickness in the world if
God were on the field. There would be no sin or death on earth
if God were on the field. It is only when you bring God to the

scene by raising up the *I* within you that you wipe out the discords of sense and bring forth divine harmony.

It is possible to bring the very presence of God to earth if you will meditate, make contact with your Center, and let that Presence be released into the world.

12) Infinite Way Principles and World Affairs

For the most part, those who have been interested in a metaphysical or spiritual approach to life have thought almost entirely in terms of what it would do for them. They have been primarily interested in whether it would heal them or their families, prosper them, or perhaps be the means of their finding some happiness, a home, or better health.

I know that you realize that those days are past. It really is not going to make any great difference whether we are sick or well, rich or poor, happy or unhappy if the world does not stay in one piece.

This, therefore, is the time when it should be comparatively easy to follow the Master and take no thought for our life because suddenly our life as an individual entity is of secondary importance. The thing that is of greatest importance now is the life of this world. We can very well accept the fact that if the world and its people survive we too will survive, but if they do not, what difference would it make if we were able to demonstrate our health and supply and the rest of the world were not around to help us enjoy it?

Today everyone who is embarked on a spiritual way of life should have a concern far greater than the demonstration of his own daily harmony, and that concern should be for the survival of the entire world. The question now is: Is there a principle of life, a spiritual principle, that will govern the world? Is there a principle which can now be relied upon to prevent the destruction of civilization and the extermination of mankind?

There can be no question but that an individual can rise so high above the immediate circumstances on earth as to make himself immune to the disasters of this world, but if that is all that is concerning him, he may find the world a lonesome place to be. This is the age in which everyone who is seriously on this Path should forget his own problems and be willing to lose his life, if need be, in the search for, and the demonstration of, that principle which will mean life for this globe. All of a sudden we are face to face with this.

It was in 1909, when the German Navy and the English Navy were lined up against each other in the North Sea, that I stood on a street in London and heard the newsboys shouting that the big European war was about to begin. As it happened, cooler heads prevailed; the situation was temporarily met; and World War I did not begin until 1914.

The thought that came into my mind that day was: Can it be possible that war is threatening these people over here, a war for which the citizens are not responsible, but a war against which they have no defense and one that could be almost completely destructive to them? The people were given no opportunity to play any decisive part as to whether the world should remain at peace or be thrust into the horrors of war. The only thing left for them to do was to pray. Nobody really believed that praying would stop a war if those in power wanted one. In fact, the world was helpless in the presence of those who were bent on destruction and personal gain.

So these thoughts came: Is it not possible that God could stop this approaching holocaust? Is there a way whereby we could bring ourselves to a place where God would intervene?

Of God, I was convinced. From my earliest days, I have felt that there must be a principle of life, a God-principle, and one that would have no sectarian connotations. This God must be universal Being, available to saint and sinner. It must be available to rich and poor, to those of any race or creed. When we discover that kind of God, we will have God on earth as It is in heaven, and we will have the means not only of restoring peace on earth, but maintaining it there forever.

DEDICATION, NECESSARY

To pray that God overcome the evil conditions on earth is a waste of time. If He has not stopped the calamities of the world in all the thousands of years past, He is not going to stop them tomorrow. This does not mean that the evil or frightening conditions on earth cannot be halted, because they can be, and they can be halted this day, this night, tomorrow morning, tomorrow night, at any time that "ten"[1] righteous men in a city will give sufficiently of themselves to realize the principles that act on earth as in heaven, that do bring forth harmony. It calls, first of all, for an understanding of those principles, but above all it calls for a dedication to the practice of them until the fruitage appears.

I would like to illustrate that in this way: There are certain diseases, and especially certain diseases to which children are subject, that do not ordinarily lend themselves to quick healing spiritually. They do not yield themselves to healing at all in

[1] Genesis 18:32.

any length of time medically, and even spiritually they seem to take time. For this reason, when those cases appear, we always suggest that the parents themselves work with practitioners or teachers, learn the principles, and learn how to pray day after day so that eventually there is a yielding of that condition and a healing. We have actually witnessed that where work is taken up for such a child for any length of time—sometimes it is a matter of months, but I have also seen it a matter of years —there is a yielding of the condition, and a return to normal in that child.

So it is with these conditions of which I am speaking in the world. It may not be that through uniting in one spiritual prayer we could stop all the discords and inharmonies and battles that are on earth in one stroke. But this is certain, if we will be diligent in giving at least one period every single day to prayer in connection with national and international affairs, we will, by the very force of our consecration and dedication, break down what is producing the discords and problems on earth.

IMPERSONALIZING THE EVILS OF THIS WORLD

There is nobody on earth responsible for evil conditions in the world. Basically, there is no one man or woman, there are no groups of men or women of the past or of the present who are responsible for the conditions that face the world today. This is a very important point to remember, and unless we come into agreement on this point our work cannot be effective. Personalizing these evils will perpetuate them.

The world is rid of the Pharaohs, the Caesars, the Ghengis Khans; the world is rid of the evil ones of the Middle Ages; the Czars are gone, Stalin is gone, Hitler is gone, and yet the evils persist and even multiply. So surely it must be evident that the solution does not lie in getting rid of whoever it is that we think is humanly responsible for our woes today.

There is no such thing as personalized evil. If you have worked with the principles of The Infinite Way, you have already proved that the impersonalization of evil is three quarters of all that is necessary for the healing. When you begin to perceive that, you are on your way to doing effective healing work because you will have stopped placing the cause of error in a person and will have placed it where it belongs: in the universal, impersonal mind of man, the carnal mind which is merely the belief in two powers, that which cast Adam and Eve out of Eden.

THE NATURE OF SPIRITUAL POWER

We are all hypnotized to some extent by the belief that there are good powers and bad powers, spiritual powers and material powers. To be dehypnotized means to come into some measure of agreement that there cannot be God and something besides God. There cannot be Spirit and something unlike or opposite to Spirit.

If you have caught the basic principles of this message, you will set aside one meditation period every day for the world, just as if this world were your patient, suffering from an incurable disease, and you were the transparency for the healing— not through one prayer, not by a single realization, but by the persistent, constant realization of your major principle, which is to recognize, as you look out at these forces that seem to be so destructive: "Thou couldest have no power at all against me, except it were given thee from above." [2] Since God is Spirit, the only operating and operative power is spiritual power.

Some forty years ago, Charles P. Steinmetz said that the

2 John 19:11.

greatest discovery of the twentieth century would be the discovery of the nature of spiritual power. And today the nature of that spiritual power is being revealed.

It has been believed by the world that spiritual power is the power of God to do something to sin, disease, death, lack, and limitation. It has been believed that spiritual power is some kind of a God-power that can be used. That is what has fooled the world. Well-meaning people have believed, and many still do, that by prayer they can bring spiritual power down to the world, and thereby remove the sins and diseases of this world. Because of this belief they have missed the way.

Spiritual power is something that is functioning at this very moment in you. You never will be able to use it; you never will know how it functions or operates: you will only be able to witness its effect in your experience, and then only when you stop trying to use it, and let it use you, let it function in you.

MOTIVE IN PRAYER

In your period of daily meditation for the world, realize that you are now uniting with all people all over the globe who are praying. Remember, however, that praying has nothing to do with what words you use or what thoughts you think: praying has to do with motive. Therefore, wherever there is an individual who is turning within with the motive of having peace revealed and established on earth, that person is in prayer. He may be praying a Catholic prayer, a Protestant prayer, a Hebrew prayer, a Vedantist prayer, or a metaphysical prayer, but the prayer is equal in effectiveness if the motive is the establishment of peace on earth. That eliminates the prayers of all those who are praying for victory, all those who are praying for their side, all those who believe that some particular kinds of prayers are more effective than others, or that a metaphysical prayer is more effective than a Protestant or Catholic prayer.

The motive of prayer must be for neither victory nor defeat: the motive of prayer must be for the establishment of peace with justice to all. When you enter prayer with that motive, the words you use or the thoughts you think are of no importance. The only way that God has of knowing us is by the motives of the heart and the intents of the mind. In other words, if what is functioning or motivating us is personal, selfish, or nationalistic, it is not prayer, and it is not reaching the throne or the consciousness of God.

Therefore, when you go into meditation for the world each day, you are of the two or more gathered together because you are uniting with persons throughout this globe who are going to the Father within and realizing:

> *Thou alone art power. Thou alone art presence. In Thy presence is fullness of life—here, there, and everywhere. In Thy presence there is only the Spirit of God, the Spirit of Love, the Spirit of Truth, the Spirit of Life, and besides this there is no other, so I am not going into meditation to use God or direct God, but to realize God.*
>
> *Here where I am, God is: there where thou art, God is; and God is Spirit, and God is Love, and besides Him there is none other.*

ATTAINING WORLD PEACE

Our duty is to know the truth. It is more than a duty: it is a privilege, and it is even more than a privilege because once we begin to see the fruitage of it, it is a great joy. As truth-students, however, this is a duty, and those who are not performing it are forfeiting a part of their own demonstration—ignorantly, but nevertheless that is what they are doing because the greatest law of prayer is the one the Master gave us: "Pray for them which despitefully use you, and persecute you; . . . For if ye love them which love you, what reward have ye?" [3]

But how do we pray for our enemies? How do we pray for world peace? Be assured of this: world peace is not going to come through the defeat of any nation or through the victory of any nation. Anyone who has any knowledge of history knows that there have always been defeats and victories, and there never yet has been peace. There never will be peace as long as there are defeats and victories. Peace cannot be achieved by anyone's defeat or by anyone's victory. Until the idea of both victory and defeat is relinquished, there will be no world peace.

Always there is with us the question of disarmament: Should we maintain so great a stockpile of bombs that other nations will fear us, and thereby peace will be attained, or should we disarm and bring about peace by that means? History has proved that neither course provides the answer. There have been periods when nations have been heavily armed, and this did not prevent a war. There have been periods when nations have disarmed, and that did not prevent war. Back in 1914, England possessed the greatest navy, in fact, the greatest concentration of arms on the face of the globe. Even this did not prevent World War I. At the beginning of World War II, England was practically without arms. This, too, did not prevent war.

A person may go around with a gun on his hip, but this will not prevent him from getting into trouble; he can go around without a gun on his hip, but that also will not prevent him from getting into trouble. It is not the presence of a gun or the absence of a gun that saves anyone, and it is not the presence of

[3] Matthew 5:44, 46.

armaments or the lack of armaments that saves a nation. The truth is that as long as the people of the world are living out from the materialistic basis that believes that either armament or disarmament will save them, the world is lost and is heading for another war.

What is the solution? Let us go back to what has been repeated again and again throughout the preceding chapters: the origin of evil. Just what is the origin of evil? The universal belief in two powers, the belief in the power of matter and the power of mind: whether it is the power of armaments or the power of tyrants' minds. When we look into history, we find that it has not always been tyrants who have brought about wars. More wars have been brought about by ignorance than by tyranny.

As truth-students, we must pray daily:

> *God alone is power. God is the law unto His universe, and that which is not ordained of God is not power. All claims of material and mental power are ignorance. That which is called mortal mind, carnal mind, the mind of tyrants, the mind of the stupid, the mind of the ignorant is not power.*
>
> *There is but one power, and because of Omnipresence, God is power everywhere on the face of the globe.*

We do not have to penetrate the Iron Curtain. God has already penetrated it. But without our conscious realization of this truth, the presence of God will not function there now any more than the presence of God has functioned there in the past. The presence of God functions only where and when there is conscious recognition and realization.

How earth-shaking it would be if only the truth-students in the world, the students of every one of the truth-movements— the unorganized teachings, and all the independent truth-teachers—would unite once a day and realize:

The place whereon I stand is holy ground. "The place whereon thou standest is holy ground." [4] *The omnipotence and omnipresence of God make of nonpower the evil intents of mankind.*

There is no power in arms or armies. Hezekiah proved that when his people came to him and warned him that the enemy was coming to attack them and outnumbered them. His response was, "With him is an arm of flesh; but with us is the Lord our God to help us, and to fight our battles." [5] And they rested in his word. They did not go out and fight. They rested in his word, and then the enemy began fighting among themselves, and the Hebrews never did have to go out into that battle.

I say unto you that this is a law and a principle. It operates in your personal life, if and as you make a daily practice of realizing:

Where I am, God is. God in the midst of me is mighty, and all those who are opposed to the purpose of God have but the "arm of flesh," or nothingness.

The Lord God in the midst of me is mighty, and there is no might external to me—not in the mind of man or the matter of man.

ATTAINING DOMINION

If you will work with these principles, you will begin to prove that that which heretofore has been resistance and opposition in your life, that which has been discordant or the source of discord, that which has been a barrier to your progress, your prosperity, or your happiness will begin to fall away.

When these principles begin to operate in your experience,

[4] Exodus 3:5.
[5] II Chronicles 32:8.

even though no one may know about it, someone will be led to you and say, "Give me help." You will not know why this person has been led to you, and he will not, but it is an inevitable occurrence. The darkness always finds the light in order that the darkness may be dispelled. When you begin to prove that God in the midst of you is omnipotence and that there is no power external to you for good or evil, in person, thing, or condition, that there is no mental or physical power that is power, for all power is given unto you, you have dominion over everything that appears in your world. The moment you begin to prove that for one neighbor or for one relative, you have sufficient Grace to do it for twenty.

By this time you will realize, "Why, this is a universal truth," and you will begin to know it for the entire world, for events as well as for people—for your community, for local and national elections, for the weather, for every person, thing, or condition that touches your life—but always in secrecy. This is a very sacred thing, and it is only in secrecy that you realize that the kingdom of God is within you.

MAINTAIN SECRECY

Always remember that the Master's teaching on prayer was to pray secretly and pray sacredly. Never voice your prayer outwardly or openly, and never let others see or know that you are praying. Make prayer a secret practice and a sacred one, and then whatever takes place within your consciousness God will bring to bear outwardly. Prayer must be like a seed buried in the ground, where nothing can reach, upset, or harm it. So your prayer, kept in secrecy within you, must be the prayer of realization:

I and the Father are one. All that the Father has is mine. Where I am, God is; where God is, I am. All power is given unto me; all dominion is given unto me. Over what and over whom? Over the belief that there are external powers.

All power is given to me through the understanding that God is Spirit, and spiritual power is the only power.

Be sure that no man knows that you are praying this prayer. Tell it to no one, except when someone comes into your experience in humility and with the desire to be taught.

Do not give this to the unprepared thought; do not try to proselyte; do not try to convince your relatives of its truth or efficacy. You cannot give truth to the human mind. Unless there is a spiritual preparedness to receive truth, you are just putting your seed in stony ground or barren soil, and nothing will come forth from it. Keep this truth as a "pearl of great price," [6] and do not show it to anybody but a connoisseur, because nobody else can appreciate it. Keep it within you, and then, abiding in this truth, praying the prayer of realization of God's grace, God's omnipotence, omniscience, omnipresence, and understanding the nonpower of what is not ordained of God, you will be fulfilling your function in this world, and you will watch the breaking up of error all over the globe and the gradual restoration of harmony.

AN UNSEEN SPIRITUAL ACTIVITY AT WORK

You are not witnessing evil on earth today. What you are witnessing is the breaking up of the evils that have been here for centuries. You are witnessing the breaking up of the old kind of capitalism that paid dividends to the few at the top and did not provide for those workers who could never save enough for their old age. You are witnessing the breaking up of the old type of homes for the poor and aged that were a blot on civilization and the breaking up of the bleak and cruel orphanages

[6] Matthew 13:46.

that were a disgrace to mankind. You are witnessing the breaking up of slavery in one country after another. You are witnessing the breaking up of bias, bigotry, prejudice, the breaking up of religious differences and the beginning of a greater unity among churches throughout the world.

You are witnessing the breaking up of conditions that have long needed correction in Africa, India, China, and Japan. All over the world you are witnessing the breaking up of the evils of absentee ownership and the controlling and exploiting of minority races and peoples. You are witnessing the breaking up of every evil about which you have read in this past century.

There is no denying that this breaking-up process is difficult. It is human nature to try to hold on to old patterns; it is human nature to try to hold on to positions that have been outgrown; it is human nature to try to hold on to the "good old days," if there ever were any such. But you see, those who try to hold on have their knuckles broken. You cannot hold on: you must let loose. Loose them and let them go! We are in a new age, in a new era, where there will be no more fighting among religious organizations, where no more will one nation try to exploit another nation. All these evils of the past are dead and gone, and the appearance of them is breaking up; and that breaking up is not easy for persons or nations.

Like anything worthwhile, however, the result of the breaking up will be greater freedom for all. If these conditions were merely breaking up because of human reasons, they would not be on quite the world-wide basis that they are. When we look upon what is going on in the world, we must remember that there is no one nation that has been or is the source of evil, nor is there one nation responsible for the evils on earth. This has been a universal belief in self-preservation: trying to attain and obtain for one's own self or one's own nation regardless of at whose expense. This belief is not a quality of any nation or any people; it is a quality and an activity of the human mind.

Therefore, the human mind, whether operating in the Occidental or the Oriental world, has been the evil. It has merely taken different forms.

If you study the history of the past twenty-five years, or if you travel—and I do not mean one of those round the world air trips on which you stop off at nineteen cities in nineteen days, but a trip which might take a year or more so that you have the opportunity to spend a week in this city, three days in that, ten days in another, a month in one country and another month in another country—you will begin to learn about the changes that have occurred in most countries in the last twenty-five years: the limitations that have been broken, the old habits and customs that have been forsaken, the old poverty that is gone forever; and you will see that what is taking place in this world today is taking place because of an unseen spiritual activity.

Behind what appears to be the wars and rumors of wars that are going on in this world, there is really a spiritual activity that is breaking the hard crust of human greed, human lust, human ambition, human pride, and restoring spiritual sonship to the entire world of mankind. Every country is giving greater and greater and greater freedom. Remember that those that are not giving greater freedom to their people, like the Iron Curtain countries, are really living on the edge of a volcano. They are maintaining themselves only by force of arms, but no one can maintain a society by force of arms forever. No one ever has!

In the days of the Czar, the people had no arms: the Czar had almost all of them, and he is gone. In every country where people have been downtrodden, they had no arms, but in the end the tyrants were routed. In the France of the eighteenth century, a revolution brought liberty, and it was not the people who had the arms; it was the government. In our own country in Revolutionary days, it was not the Colonists who had the ammunition and ships, but despite that, freedom came.

Never believe for a moment that freedom is dependent on arms or ammunition. Freedom is dependent on an individual's realization of God and the nonpower of whatever it is that appears as an enslaving or limiting power. If you admit anything at all as a power of limitation, you make that limitation a law unto yourself. To be free of lack, to be free of discord, to be free of inharmony, abide in the truth of God as the only Reality, the only Presence, and the only Power, and abide in the truth that the source of every form of evil, the source of every form of limitation is the "arm of flesh," or nothingness.

ABIDE IN ONE POWER

Do not look upon evil as opposing good: there is no such thing. Do not believe that Truth overcomes evil: there is no such thing. See Truth as infinite, and evil as the "arm of flesh," and you will bring forth harmony in your experience. Do not accept a God that has to battle sin, disease, death, tyranny, or anything else. Accept a God infinite in nature, omnipresent in being, omnipotent in action, and then look out at all the temptations and the tempters of the world:

> *Thou hast only the "arm of flesh," nothingness. I abide in this word: God in the midst of me is the only power. Where God is realized, there is power for neither good nor evil.*
>
> *All power is given unto me. All power is embodied in the Christ, the son of God, which in truth I am. The son of God is lifted up in me out of the tomb of material sense. This is the resurrection. This is the ascension.*

Lift up this son of God in you and realize:

> *He that is within me is greater than any thing, or any belief, or any power in the universe. He that is within me is the All-*

*power, and that which is external to me and not ordained of
God is not power and is not presence. God, Spirit, is the only
power—not mind and not matter. God is law, therefore Spirit
is the only law with power.*

The fact that these statements represent truth will not save
you. "Ye shall know the truth, and the truth shall make you
free." [7] You must abide in this truth, dwell in it, live in it, hour
by hour, day by day, and night by night, until it is a very part
of your being, and then all of a sudden a spiritual light dawns
within you, and it comes to you, " 'Whereas I was blind, now I
see.' [8] Now I know that Spirit is really the substance of all
form, the law of all form, the cause of all form. My error has
been that I have been believing in a power outside, a power in
form, a power in thought, whereas all power is spiritual
power."

As you abide in the Word, remember always that there is
still one more step, and that is, after contemplating the truth
about God, to be still and listen:

*"Speak, Lord; for thy servant heareth." [9] Thou utterest Thy
voice, the earth melteth.*

Error is not in the external; power is not in the external; all
power is in "still small voice." [10] There is no power in sin, no
power in disease, no power in tyrants, no power in external
conditions: power is in the still small voice.

As you abide in stillness, eventually you come to that place
where a release takes place within you, and then you will know
that God is on the scene, and your work is finished. You have
opened out a way for "the imprisoned splendor" to escape. The

[7] John 8:32.
[8] John 9:25.
[9] I Samuel 3:9.
[10] I Kings 19:12.

power that is within you now becomes the power in your world. Your world may be limited to your own family, or you may eventually accept the entire world as your world, and let your consciousness of truth govern this entire world.

In the midst of threatening world conditions, I say to you: Think in higher terms than your own health, your own supply, or your own happiness. For some part of every day give yourself to the realization and the practice of these principles through which you have witnessed healings of minor or major problems, principles that have helped you or your neighbors, and begin now to think in terms of a principle revealing itself on earth as the presence of God, universally.